Hendrix

19.

Don

© Copyright 1972 Chris Welch
© Copyright 1973 Flash Books, New York
© Copyright 1978 Quick Fox, New York
This edition published 1982 by Omnibus Press
(A division of Book Sales Limited)
© Copyright 1982 Omnibus Press

Exclusive distributors:
Book Sales Limited
8/9 Frith Street, London, W1V 5TZ, England

Music Sales Pty. Ltd.
120 Rothschild Avenue,
Rosebery, NSW 2018, Australia.

ISBN 0.7119.0144.9
OP 41987

For Marilyne

Designed by Pearce Marchbank

The author would like to thank the
following for their help and cooperation
in the preparation of this book:
Chas Chandler, Jim Gray, Noel Redding,
Jeanette Jacobs, Monika Danneman,
Gary Stickells, Ray Coleman, Eric Barrett,
Keith Altham, and Miles.

Hendrix
A Biography by Chris Welch

Omnibus Press
London/New York/Sydney

Hendrix

Designed by Pearce Marchbank

Hey Jimi

Many are convinced that the Jimi Hendrix Story is a tragedy. Either his life or death — was a tragedy. But it seems more a tragedy of errors and misunderstanding, foolishness and lack of communication. Jimi was not a tragic figure. The sadness at a waste of life and talent should not cloud the fact that Jimi's death was an accident, as avoidable as the nonsense that frequently pursued his career.

Jimi was full of energy and humour. He sought after experience and enjoyed living. He jumped from aeroplanes, tried drugs and relished women. His problems were largely those that beset many others who found fame and success in the rock music phenomenon of the 'sixties. He was not an innocent, or a fool, but he was unprepared for the shifting values and unrealities that rock and roll stardom presents.

His other problems stemmed from a disjointed childhood, scarred by the death of his mother. He found it difficult to trust people, perhaps because he had been disappointed too many times.

He could be gentle, boyish, and witty. At other times he could be explosive, violent and hard. As a girlfriend explained: 'He would play stupid — just to see how far people would go with him. He was a joker, but he could get mad at people.'

Were drugs important? Were friends real? Were his music and his image honest? Jimi must have asked himself a lot of questions during his period of exile after the original Experience broke up. It may have been that Jimi was finding some of the answers just before he died.

As a rock hero Jimi was one of the best, one of the greatest. Lying on his back playing flaming guitar with his teeth. Fantastic! He looked mean, slick and ugly. He was outrageous in a Bob Dylan hairstyle, gaudy clothes, a sly smile, tongue licking nervously over his lips. Young girls were supposed to scream. Yet Jimi appealed to young white boys who came looking for outrage, rebellion, and the best blues guitar they ever heard.

Certainly in England, his adopted home, the hard core of his audience were young blues and rock fans, aged between 15 and 25, who loved Jimi for his stage dash and flash and admired his virtuoso electric guitar work. They liked the whole Experience, the bombastic yet sophisticated drums of Mitch Mitchell and the sympathetic bass of Noel Redding.

They made a brilliant team. But almost from the start there were cracks in the superstructure that would contribute to the downfall of both edifice and architect.

Although Cream were the forerunners of the three man virtuoso rock group and pioneers of what degenerated into so-called 'heavy' music, the Jimi Hendrix Experience stole a lot of their thunder and gained much quicker acceptance. Their music was more spectacular, less predictable and it splashed into the rainbow colours of 1967 psychedelia with gay abandon.

In another time Jimi would have played in working man's obscurity, and would then have been investigated and documented as one of the great natural blues performers, hailed as another Robert Johnson, impoverished and a discographer's delight.

But Jimi was destined to be a rock star, highly paid, idolised, romanticised, publicised. 'How's that?' he asks with eager nervousness after cutting his '67 version of 'Red House' on the album *Are you Experienced*.

'Yeah', comes a slightly surprised voice from the talk-back, it was just another 12-bar jam wasn't it?

But it was a beautiful blues performance, powerful, fluent, twisting like an eel and full of funk. It seemed nobody could quite reassure Jimi that he was a fine singer, writer, player. Many could see no further than the smoke of a burning guitar.

It seemed then that Jimi's career with the revolutionary English pick-up group had limitless possibilities. It was the time of the Beatles' Sgt. Pepper album, such a big influence on record makers — Jimi included. The vibes were right for experiment. *Are You Experienced* was in the same league as *Strawberry Fields Forever* and all the other acid-inspired delving into backward tapes and the whole armoury of studio effects.

But all the promises of '67 seemed to fade after a couple of unique albums and some extraordinary tours, and there was to be no real fulfilment, artistically, until the release of the *Cry Of Love* **after** Jimi's death.

Fans continued to cheer, but the Experience which faltered through a concert at London's Royal Albert Hall in 1969 and at the Isle of Wight in 1970 was not the same explosive, brilliant team that stunned London in 1966.

What went wrong? In later chapters those who knew and loved him give us clues in their reminiscenses to the man behind the image. A pattern emerges of a musician who at first accepted the format of an imposed popular image, largely engineered by the traditional methods of showbusiness, but later came to resent and reject the demands made on him.

Jimi loved playing to audiences and there's no doubt he was thoroughly determined to succeed as well as to experiment and improve his music. But the pressures on him to maintain the magic of the hit-maker could not be shaken off.

Right up to his death he often mentioned a dream he had for a big band setting, with vocal backing that would help him work out new ideas on stage. He always felt a responsibility to the fans who were expecting him to play guitar with his teeth or kick over his amplifiers, but he had long grown beyond the showmanship of '67. The sorry truth was that he had nothing to replace it on stage, and he couldn't find the right collaborators to help him develop the quality of his music.

As rock music progressed at a phenomenal rate, it just wasn't enough to stand on stage and jam anymore. For those who had ears to what was happening, or rather not happening, most of his latter concerts proved anti-climactic.

At the Isle of Wight Festival in 1970 Jimi made his last British appearance. Thousands waited in the dark, damp fields until the early hours of Sunday morning, waiting for the equipment to be set up and tested, waiting for Jimi to appear. When he came on, a great surge of expectancy came through the crowd pressed in front of the light-bathed stage. It was about 3 a.m., cold and starry skied. 'Yes, it has been a long time, hasn't it?' said Jimi in his hip drawl,

An Introduction

smiling down.

Jimi started to play well, but the music quickly seemed to lose direction and the first numbers received only polite applause. 'Let's start all over again,' he said quickly. 'Hello, England.' The conviction grew that nothing was going to happen we hadn't heard before.

It was cold and late and tiring. So I left, and began the long walk back through moonlit country lanes to a distant hotel. Over the fields for miles distant, Jimi could be heard singing and his guitar wailing. A roar of applause seemed to greet him, like the murmuring of the sea against the nearby cliffs. We wouldn't see Jimi again.

The suggestion has been made that if Jimi had lived he would just have gone down and down, a travesty of his own legend. But if he could revitalise his recording activity with the *Cry Of Love*, it should not be ruled out that Jimi could have entered a bright and productive new era of public performing. His guitar artistry was still there, and the speed of his playing on 'Johnny B. Goode' on the *Hendrix In The West* album was evidence of his remarkable flexibility. But he needed a stronger working framework, a greater challenge than just bass and drums.

The impact of this sad farewell at the 1970 festival contrasted with the happier memory of his first appearances in London. Chas Chandler, Jimi's co-manager with Mike Jeffery, had not been long out of the Animals. He had given up bass guitar and Newcastle Brown ale to become a tycoon. At least that was the plan. He bought a suit and he found an act.

The act was Jimi, whom he had seen working in New York. He brought him to London, and the first faint recollection of meeting him was a nervous 'Hello' at a party in some long-forgotten flat. Jimi sat on the floor in a corner and didn't say anything. Nobody seemed to say much to him either. It was December 1966, and Christmas was coming up. A stream of club parties made the days merge into a blur. Meanwhile at a new club in East London called the Upper Cut, the Who were battering out 'My Generation'.

From the Upper Cut it was a short drive to Blaises, a basement club in Queensgate, London, where musicians, agents, managers, and writers allowed themselves to be deafened whilst imbibing quantities of alchohol. Chas's first signing was going to make his debut, and already his reputation had spread like wildfire among the ranks of club-goers. The club was packed and the only way to see Jimi was to stand on tip-toe and crane the neck. In the squashed and steaming crush around the pocket-sized stage, I glimpsed my first sighting of Jimi Hendrix, and scribbled 'Jimmy Hendricks', on my inkstained notebook.

'What's that number called Chas?' I demanded as each tune came blasting inches from the eardrums.

Jimi stood crouched over his guitar, rocking back and forth in the few square feet normally reserved for boogalooing. When he lifted up his guitar to his teeth and noises screeched from the amplifiers it seemed almost frightening. It was expected that blood would fleck from his lips or volts of electricity would course through his body. It was altogether disturbing, and the mixture of styles seemed odder still. Nearly all black artists either played jazz or sang soul. Jimi was blowing rock with a flavour of Bob Dylan and the screeching feedback of the Who.

He may have looked incredible as well, but in the crowd of eager guitarists — they included Pete Townshend and Jeff Beck — it was almost impossible to see him.

Later in the Melody Maker there appeared a brief 'Caught In The Act' review: 'Jimi Hendrix, a fantastic American guitarist blew the minds of the star-packed crowd who went to see him at Blaises. Jimi's trio blasted through some beautiful sounds like 'Rock Me Baby', 'Third Stone From The Sun', 'Like A Rolling Stone', 'Hey Joe' and even an unusual version of the Trogg's 'Wild Thing'. Jimi has great stage presence and an exceptional guitar technique, which involves playing with his teeth on occasions and no hands on others! Jimi looks like becoming one of the big club names of '67.'

Some days later, just after Christmas, it seemed most of London went to see Jimi again, this time at the Bag O'Nails, a club run by Rik and Johnny Gunnell near Carnaby Street. It was packed with rock stars, seated at long tables in front of the stage. Apart from the impact Jimi was making, Mitch's drumming came as a great surprise as well. He had been playing swing style jazz drums with Georgie Fame most of the previous year, and now he seemed to be going berserk, rolling around in his kit in unheard-of fashion.

The next night everybody went again to see Jimi and the Experience, this time at the opening of a new club, the short-lived 7½ just off Piccadilly. The audience, sweltering but determined not to miss a note, included Mick Jagger, Marianne Faithfull, Pete Townshend, Eric Clapton, Anita Pallenberg, Fenella Fielding, and the Misunderstood — an American band with steel guitarist Glenn Campbell.

Once again Jimi's effect on audiences, consisting largely of musicians not exactly easy to impress, was staggering. And it wasn't long before the ·Experience was shared with the public when the group took off on the extraordinary pop tour of Spring '67, billed with Engelbert Humperdinck, Cat Stevens and the Walker Brothers.

There was· also a concert at Brian Epstein's Saville Theatre, a marvellous venture that brought some memorable rock bills to the heart of London's theatre belt. When Jimi Hendrix played there with the Who, it seemed likely the building would collapse.

Reported the Melody Maker: 'Jimi Hendrix v. The Who! It was a close battle at London's Saville Theatre on Sunday. And fans will still be arguing about the winners. Either way, two of Britain's most exciting groups thrilled the crowds with hard-hitting sounds and sights. After the Koobas came the Experience. And what an Experience! Jimi was hit by PA trouble, but the crowd were so keyed up they· laughed sympathetically while Jimi searched for a mike that worked. The incredible 'Wild Thing' ended in a freak out of guitar biting, feed-back and uproar. Follow that — was the feeling.'

Once again the stars turned out, and the Sunday concert was attended by Steve Marriott, John Lennon, Paul McCartney,

Spencer Davis, Michael D'Abo, Klaus Voorman, Eric Clapton, Jack Bruce, and Lulu.

The Walker Brothers tour was incredible. On the opening night at the Astoria, Finsbury Park, Jimi first set fire to his guitar. I had been in the dressing room with them before the show started, but nothing was given away about the plot involving a match and some lighter fuel.

'Jimi Hendrix was hit by amplifier trouble, and while he was visually exciting, his guitar could not be heard above the drumming of Mitch Mitchell.

'They wore beautifully coloured stage gear, almost as bright as the flames which leapt ten feet from Jimi's guitar at the end of his act. Unfortunately Jimi and compere Nick Jones were both burnt in the accident and a fire extinguisher had to be rushed on stage, while the audience yelled in surprise.'

My surprise equalled that of the audience, and it wasn't until a year later we heard about the lighter fuel.

Jimi was warned by the tour organisers to 'clean up his act'. The first hint of sexuality had already crept into the stage act, but probably the actual cause of friction was the attempts by the Hendrix camp to upstage the rest of the show.

The great days of the Jimi Hendrix Experience were already over in a matter of months. From then on, whenever I saw them, a steady decline had set in. Those first gigs at the London discos were tight, explosive and fresh. Later the band became ragged, loose and aimless. They seemed to suffer enormous problems with amplification, and at one Saville Theatre appearance they were completely unable to cope when an amplifier blew out.

There was an agonising wait while it was being repaired, and then Mitch's drums, which were miked up, were distorted and deafening. The Experience were a proving ground for the bigger sound systems that were to come. It was unfortunate that the linking of individual amplifiers with a separate PA system and the placing of a sound engineer with a mixing console at the rear of the auditorium to constantly check and balance the sound, had not arrived.

While the Experience gained their first few single hits, and wandered into album recording, it seemed to me that the band were falling apart, and that no strong new direction could take them on from 'Wild Thing' and 'Hey Joe'.

When the group reached its peak, with fans in Britain and America screaming for them and Jimi being hailed with Stateside slogans like 'the Black Elvis', they were trapped into an exhausted formula which had to be maintained at all costs.

The personalities closest to Jimi were obviously Mitch Mitchell and Noel Redding. There were also his road managers, men like Eric Barrett, Gerry Stickells and others. There was Chas Chandler, the ex-Animal, whose partner, Mike Jeffery, later took a keener interest as manager.

It is repeatedly stated by many who knew him that 'Jimi had few friends.' This may have stemmed from a fear of becoming too closely attached to someone and risking being hurt. And yet there is no dearth of people who had dealings with him who liked, respected and even loved him. Jimi loved to jam, and he played with musicians like Eric Clapton, Stephen Stills, Steve Winwood and Dave Mason. There were his American friends, drummer Buddy Miles and bassist Billy Cox.

All who worked with him emphasise Jimi's charm. Some like Tony Garland, his first public relations man, were struck by his humour. 'He was incredibly shy and terribly polite, but he had a great sense of humour. He was one of the nicest geezers I've ever met, yet he was promoted as a monster. He used to have a lot of private jokes. He'd tell a story and make people believe it. Then he'd say "Woof woof" — to let people know he was lying. That was called selling a Woof Ticket to someone. He could also do a great Harlem queen impression that was really funny.'

There were those who claim that Jimi was over-worked, made to tour, kept filled with drugs to make him 'manageable', and generally exploited. It is suggested that his image was entirely fabricated, that he was twisted and torn by black power interests, and a picture is painted of him ultimately reduced to a mindless wreck.

There are elements of truth in this, but too often people have been quick to project their own imagined grievances and make Jimi an example of their own plight. 'I've got problems too man. It's just like what they did to Jimi.'

How easily facts can be misinterpreted was demonstrated to me when a woman friend expressed her sorrow and indignation at the way Jimi appeared backstage at his Isle of Wight concert. 'He was over-worked totally and people neglected him. There was a heavy responsibility on the people around him to look after him that was not taken. At the Isle of Wight, it was heart-breaking. He'd been up all night without sleep.'

Yet road manager Eric Barrett in his cheery reminiscences recalls that he and Jimi had flown to the gig straight after a wild party in New York for the opening of the Electric Lady studio. 'We had a ball,' said Eric.

If he was hustled by the Black Power movement, who perhaps disliked seeing a Black American musician working with white English musicians and appealing to white audiences, then he could doubtless handle them with his logic and charm. Singer Jeanette Jacobs recalls an incident when Jimi was being urged to buy a painting that would raise funds for such an organisation. 'He just said — you do your thing man, and I'll do mine.' For Jimi was metaphorically colour blind and found it difficult to comprehend prejudice, let alone discuss it.

He took drugs and probably enjoyed them. He was not a hard-drug addict, but like most artists or creative people, he needed stimulation. His success came at a time when LSD was making its fantastic impact on young people in America and Europe. Like a large percentage of rock musicians, he experimented with it heavily. Perhaps it is to his credit that he kept drugs under control in such a potentially dangerous environment.

None of his problems were insoluble, and his intelligence could not have let despair dominate him, however recurrent the bouts of loneliness and frustration. Jimi Hendrix just needed more time. But time was not on his side.

Rise, Fall & Rise

Jimi Hendrix was James Marshall Hendrix, born in Seattle, Washington, November 27, 1942. It was a town he didn't particularly like and rarely cared to visit. He was the son of a landscape gardener, Mr. James Allen Hendrix, and he grew up in a predominantly white community, attending white schools.

His mother, Lucille, who died when he was young, was of Indian descent, and Jimi spent a lot of his childhood going up to Vancouver to stay with his grandmother, who was a full-blooded Cherokee.

Said Jimi: 'My mother and father used to fall out a lot and I always had to be ready to go tippy-toeing off to Canada. My dad was level-headed and religious, but my mother used to like having a good time and dressing up. She used to drink a lot and didn't take care of herself. She died when I was about ten. But she was a groovy mother.'

Jimi went to Garfield High School, Seattle, but left when he was 16. He once said he had been thrown out for 'holding a white girl's hand in class.' But he also had to leave school because his wage earning capacity was needed. 'Dad was a gardener and it got pretty bad in the winter when there wasn't any grass to cut.'

James and Lucille Hendrix had another son, Leon, 5 years younger than Jimi. He, too, plays the guitar. After Lucille died, James Hendrix remarried, and has two daughters by his second marriage.

Mr. Hendrix believed that the first time Jimi became interested in music was when he was about ten years old. He used to pretend that the household broom was a guitar, and told his dad he was 'learning how to play it.' So when Jimi was eleven, Dad bought him a cheap acoustic, and at 12 he gave him his first electric guitar.

After Jimi had joined the army, his family did not hear from him for a long time, until he 'phoned his father in September 1966, to say he was in England and they were going to make him a star. 'We've changed my name to Jimi,' said the erstwhile Jimmy. And he explained it was 'just to be different . . .' Said Mr. Hendrix: 'We were both so excited, I forgot to even tell him I'd remarried.'

'My dad was very strict and taught me that I must respect my elders always. I couldn't speak unless I was spoken to first

Jimi Hendrix with Curtis Knight and The Squires in the early sixties.

by grown ups. So I've always been very quiet. But I saw a lot of things. A fish wouldn't get into trouble if he kept his mouth shut.'

Jimi had no musical education and learnt to play guitar at school and in the army. He listened to records and watched other guitar players. The blues was naturally his greatest influence and he listened to Elmore James, B.B. King and Muddy Waters. He also liked Bob Dylan. It was this latter influence that was to prove important in the development of Jimi's unique musical attitude.

Most black musicians gravitated towards the formal restrictions of the showbiz styled Tamla Motown vocal groups, or the stand up balladeering. Jimi was the first black rock artist, in the sense that he combined the desire to say something in his lyrics other than the usual soul hallelujahs, while retaining all the grit of a natural blues player. Jimi had good reason to be tired of soul and all its machine-like girations. Later he was to have a basin full of working on the soul circuits as a backing guitarist.

Neither of Jimi's parents were musicians, but Jimi used to relate: 'My dad danced and played the spoons. My first instrument was a harmonica which I got when I was about four, I suppose. Next it was a violin. I always dug string instruments and pianos. Then I started digging guitars — it was the instrument that always seemed to be around. Everybody's house you went into seemed to have one lying around. I was about 14 or 15 when I started playing guitar and I remember my first gig was at an armoury, a National Guard place, and we earned 35 cents apiece. In those days I just liked rock and roll I guess. We used to play stuff by people like the Coasters. Anyway, you all had to do the same things before you could join a band — you all even had to do the same steps.'

In 1963, he joined the US army, and the 101st Airborne. Said Jimi: 'I figured I'd have to go sooner or later, so I volunteered to get it over with so I could get my music together later on. And when I joined I figured I might as well go all the way, so I joined the airborne. I hated the army immediately.' In the paratroops, Jimi made 25 jumps, and was injured on his 26th and discharged. What made him do parachute jumps?

'The sergeant,' laughed Jimi. 'And the fact you got more money. Did I get any pleasure from it? More like a thrill. The pleasure came when you found you had landed safely. Anyway I was lucky to get out when I did. Vietnam was just coming up.

'I had no music training so I couldn't sign up as a musician. But I did play here and there. Anyway, when I got out I didn't have anything to show for it all, so I wasn't going home.'

After his 14 month stint in the army, Jimi spent a lot of time on the road, playing with different bands from Nashville to Los Angeles.

'I was trying to play my own thing, but I was working with people like Little Richard, the Isley Brothers and Wilson Pickett and they didn't like too much of that feedback. I was always kept in the background but I was thinking all the time about what I wanted to do. I used to join a group and quit them so fast. They were mostly what you might call R&B groups. I dug listening to Top 40 R&B but that doesn't necessarily mean I like to play it every night.'

Jimi worked on some star-packed tours backing B.B. King, Sam Cooke, Solomon Burke, Chuck Jackson, and Jackie Wilson. And he also worked for Ike and Tina Turner, Little Richard, the Isley Brothers and the famous twist band, Joey Dee and the Starlighters.

'I learned how not to get an R&B band together. The trouble was too many leaders didn't seem to want to pay anybody. Guys would get fired in the middle of the highway because they were talking too loud on the bus or the leader owed them too much money — something like that. The first real group I got together on my own was back in Greenwich Village. That would be around 1965 I guess. I changed my name to Jimmy James and called the group the Blue Flames — not exactly original was it?

'I had no doubts about coming to England. I'd never been and thought I'd take a look, and I didn't feel I was ready to play all over the States.'

Talking about his influences, he said: 'When I first started I liked anything from B.B. King to Muddy Waters, Bach to Eddie Cochran. But I didn't try to copy anybody. Those were just the people that gave me the feeling to get my own thing together. Then before I came to England I was digging a lot of the things Bob Dylan was doing. When I first heard him I thought: "You must admire that guy for having that much nerve to sing so out of key." But then I listened to the words. My own thing is in my head. I hear sounds and if I don't get them together, nobody else will.'

There are various recorded examples of Jimi's guitar playing around this time, with the Isley Brothers and Curtis Knight, but Jimi was never particularly proud of them, and didn't like to see them reissued. Attempts were made to stop some of the Curtis Knight releases, which reappeared after Jimi had become successful with the Experience.

In 1967 he said: 'They were nothing but jam sessions man, with a group called the Squires. No, I didn't sing on "Hush Now" that was dubbed on later by someone trying to copy my voice. And on that one the guitar was out of tune and I was stoned out of my mind. We're going to get those records stopped.'

There is some recorded evidence of his early experiments on tape recordings made at Mike Ephron's New York apartment in Autumn 1964. They are mainly jams given titles like 'Feels Good', 'Frid Cola', etc. which were released in three volumes by Saga. But the title *Jimi Hendrix at his Best* is not exactly fair, as they are the kind of blowing sessions that most musicians would rather not let their audiences hear.

John Hammond Jnr. son of the famous jazz and blues critic, and a singer and guitarist in his own right, remembered hearing Jimi play in Greenwich Village in 1966:

'When I first met Jimi he was destitute. He had even been robbed of his guitar. I think it was in October when I was playing at a club called the Gaslight. Across the street was the Cafe Wha, a really funky joint. Jimi was playing there, and I went by one night. He was playing some of my songs off an album. He was incredible-looking and seemed pleased to meet me. I asked him how I could help, and he said: 'Get me a gig. Get me out of here!' So I got him a gig at the Cafe A Go Go and I worked there with him for a month with Jimi playing lead guitar. Bob Dylan, the Beatles and the Stones all came by to watch us play. Then he had offers to go to England from Chas Chandler. He went. I saw him afterwards and he had become a superstar.'

In London at that time, whatever the Beatles or Stones said about an artist or style of music was accepted as gospel, and in many ways John Lennon, Paul Mc-Cartney and Mick Jagger did a lot in their enthusiasm for artists like Bob Dylan, James Brown — and Jimi Hendrix, in getting them recognition and acceptance in England.

Jimi was nervous about coming to England, but the way was already being cleared. The music press were informed, friends alerted, and when Jimi arrived in London he was first taken to the home of Zoot Money, the bandleader and looner, who quickly made Jimi welcome with a jam at Gunterstone Road, just off the Cromwell Road.

His impact on club audiences in London was not a faked or hyped excitement. Nothing like it had ever been seen before, and bearing in mind the band hardly had time to rehearse before giving their first concert with Johnny Halliday in Paris, all the flash and showmanship was Jimi's. And naturally, managers Chas Chandler and Mike Jeffery, were keen to exploit and emphasise Jimi's sensational appeal.

In fact the band were never exactly over-rehearsed and it is obvious now that the electrifying 'newness' held it all together. As soon as the nightly routine began to pall, that's when the band began to fall apart. And the rest of Jimi's years in England and in the States were spent searching for an alternative.

Jimi's first single and first hit 'Hey Joe' was released 16th December, 1966. By the time his first British tour opened at the Finsbury Park Astoria, on March 31, 1967, 'Hey Joe' had already established Jimi as the titular head of the 'underground', at least in terms of whose posters and albums should be most prominently displayed in one's pad. And he had become a figure of great

controversy in a country only just learning to live with Lennon and Jagger. With his beaming smile and gorgeous clothes he was a highly sought-after fashion figure, vying with Nureyev and Jagger for space on the glossy magazine covers. Jimi's clothes were copied, discussed and admired. Even Mitch and Noel found themselves photographed and feted. It didn't have much to do with music, but it guaranteed the group coverage on TV and in the national newspapers.

Naturally enough, there were plenty who viewed them with a distaste almost amounting to fear. Sometimes it was hard for them to get taxis, or service in restaurants. In June, 1967, the group claimed that thirty hotels in Stockholm banned them and they had to fly on to Helsinki, Finland, where a night club refused them admittance.

'I have been watching Top of the Pops,' said one viewer of this popular television programme in a letter to the *Sunday Sun* 'and believe me if I had to give a cup to the leading nitwits of the programme it would be between the Move and Jimi Hendricks group.

'The first lot were absolutely stupid. I am sure the drummer must have suffered from the itch or something. As for the Hendrick's group, I hope I never meet any of them in the dark, with their hair sticking out like huge mops.

'Hendricks himself looks awful because of the way he dresses. Heaven preserve us from such. I know it takes all sorts to make a world, but do they ever take a long look at themselves?' *Disgusted Viewer, Newcastle-on-Tyne, May 14, 1967.*

Not even pop fans could always find appreciation of Hendrix's music easy. Wrote one John Dickin, of Shefford, Beds., to the New Musical Express in May 1967:

'How on earth did "Purple Haze" by Jimi Hendrix get into the charts? Hendrix and his group are an insult to pop music and the sooner the record buying public wakes up to this fact the better. Such records are nothing but a lot of noise and have no musical value whatsoever.'

Such dogmatic statements from ruffled readers are very familiar to the staffs of music newspapers. But somtimes even the critics failed to remain objective when it came to the wildest sound in rock.

'The kindest thing I could say about the Jimi Hendrix Experience in *Are You Experienced* is that I survived one full session, although it took me some time to assure myself that nothing had gone wrong with the stylus. A refreshing return to normality is provided by Liverpool's Swinging Blue Jeans . . .' George Gregson, *Liverpool Post,* June 1967.

'I can think of no-one I know who likes Jimi Hendrix's appearance, and I'm not all

rock was hardly of interest to small girls who looked upon Davey Jones as an extension of their teddy bear. It was obvious the band had to be dropped before they broke up in disgust. And to cover it up a story was concocted that is still freely quoted. As Chas Chandler admits, it was unlikely the Daughters of the American Revolution had ever heard of Jimi Hendrix, yet they were blamed for protesting at his 'indecent' stage gestures and getting him 'banned'.

It was this episode that strained the relationship between the management partners Chandler and Jeffery, and must have embarrassed Hendrix in his own country.

Says Eric Burdon, who had been Chas Chandler's colleague in the Animals: 'It was the return to America that had a lot to do with Jimi's downer trip. When you escape from the ghetto it's a mistake to go back. Jimi was a prince abroad, but when he returned to the streets he knew, he went through a lot of changes.'

Nevertheless they remained hot through '67 and their concerts at London's first rock theatre, the Saville, run by Brian Epstein, were sensational. It was on August 27 that Beatles' manager Epstein died suddenly from an overdose of sleeping tablets. The news came to the Saville during Hendrix first house and the second set was cancelled as a mark of respect, much to the chagrin of fans waiting outside. Most people agreed that Brian would probably have preferred the show to have gone on. But Jimi played the theatre again on October 8, with Arthur Brown.

My memory of these Saville concerts was one of fire that came in fits and starts. Frequently the equipment would break down, or the sound was bad. But those short, sharp 45 minute acts of long ago had

Opposite: Hendrix with Mick Jagger
Above: A publicity shot later used as a poster.

Opposite: Hendrix on stage in Seattle, Washington–his home town.

more lasting impact than all the three-hour rock shows joined together.

One of the first big all-star rock concerts in Britain came with the Christmas On Earth concert on December 22, at London's Olympia. Jimi appeared with the Pink Floyd, the Move and the Who. Later most of the musicians from the show, which was not a financial success, went to the Speakeasy Club, already established as the hipsters' hang-out. There Jimi jammed until the early hours of the morning, and for years Jimi would be a frequent guest on stage at informal blowing sessions.

Early in 1968 Jimi and the group were booked for a three day trip to Sweden. It resulted in an episode that confirmed the suspicions of the general public and hotel managers that pop stars were not to be trusted. It was an unfortunate incident, that may have glamourised Jimi in the eyes of his fans but which had a chastening effect on him. Years later he was to refer to his experiences in the song 'My Friend' on the *Cry Of Love* album,

It happened at the Opelan Hotel in Gothenburg. On January 4 it was announced that he had been held by the police for 12 hours after 'damaging his hotel room.' Photographs appeared of Jimi, head bowed, accompanied by the local fuzz who had been called by the hotel management. His passport was impounded and Jimi slept the night in jail. It was said that he was drunk. When he woke up he said he was sorry and would pay for the damage. On January 12 he was charged in Gothenburg with destroying furnishings worth £475. Reports said: 'He is alleged to have played drums in his room, then smashed windows, mirrors and chairs. During the night hotel staff and guests heard screams coming from Hendrix' room. Police

Above: Hendrix visiting his father, step-mother and brother Leon in Seattle.

Opposite: A West Coast shop-front.

said they arrested Hendrix after three of his colleagues sat on him to calm him down.'

When Chas Chandler went to see him in jail Jimi told him he couldn't remember anything about what happened. He was released, but had to pay a fine that represented all his earnings in Sweden.

At the end of January Jimi set off with a caravan of British groups on a two month tour of America. With the Experience went the Animals, Alan Price, the Soft Machine and Eire Apparent. It should have been the beginning of a new stage of success for the Experience, but reports filtered back to England indicating all was not well. A review of their Anaheim Convention Centre concert in February 1968 said: 'Jimi's show was dissappointing. His wild singing and dancing were noticeably absent. And he blew an amplifier and played only four numbers on the second show.'

It seemed that already Jimi was tiring of the flaming guitars and string-biting routines, so heavily stylised yet so much in demand.

During 1968, the *Electric Ladyland* double album was released. There was immediate controversy about the cover design, which featured a fleshy display of young ladies, who were and probably still are, extremely attractive, but by the skill of the photographer were made to look remarkably debauched.

Nevertheless, the music contained some gems, including the 'Burning Of The Midnight Lamp', 'All Along the Watchtower', 'Voodoo Chile' and the intriguing '1983 (A Merman I Should Turn To Be)'.

The music was much looser than it had ever been before, and the generous playing-time of a double album gave plenty of room for jamming in the studio. 'Voodoo Chile' was one of the best rock jams of the era

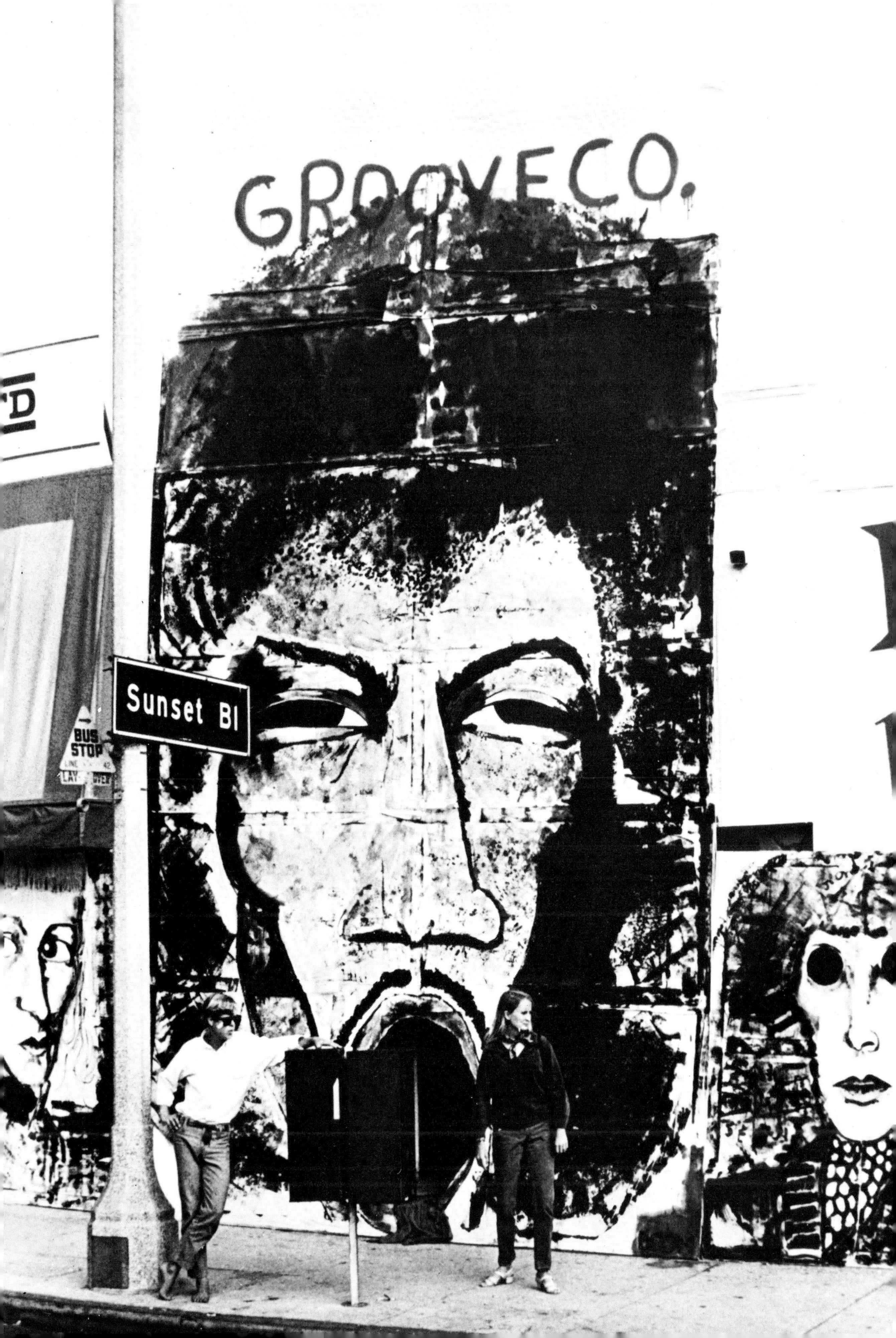

GROOVECO.
Sunset Bl
BUS STOP

Above: Billy Cox talking to Hendrix as they wait to play at the Isle of Wight, 1970, Hendrix's last major public appearance.

when rock musicians began to follow in the footsteps of their jazz forebears and improvise at length.

It was during the cutting of this album in New York that Chas Chandler felt the squeeze was on, and bowed out of operations leaving Jimi to produce it himself. He was obviously itching to experiment, but it was equally obvious, and borne out by his remarks elsewhere, that Noel Redding was not so keen on spending hours in the studio.

At the time, many found the double set a disappointment, a messy kind of self-indulgence lacking the compact brilliance and fire of the first two albums. But there was a great deal of fine guitar work from Jimi, particularly on 'Voodoo Chile'. Mitch's drumming was as bright and busy as ever, and there were studio guests of the calibre of Steve Winwood to add to the sense of occasion.

The album opened with Jimi's beloved studio effects, burbling and echoing, leading in the gentle and almost soulful 'Electric Ladyland' title. It was here that Jimi felt his voice was improving, and girlfriend Jeanette Jacobs who was in the studio recalls: 'Jimi began jumping up and down during the playback saying: "I can sing, I can sing!" It's Jeanette's voice, incidentally, that can be heard complaining about the bar being shut at the end of the jam session track.

'Cross Town' was a nice and funky track, with Jimi singing in his best declaiming style. This fades into the atmospheric 'Voodoo Chile' with Jimi singing unison riffs with his guitar in the best blues tradition.

Hearing the album again after an interval of a few years, it sounds infinitely better than it did on release to ears thirsting for a new 'Hey Joe' or 'Foxy Lady'. And Noel Redding proves he did have a writing contribution to make to the music with 'Little Miss Strange', his chirpy composition that opens side two. There is a down home funky feel to 'Long Hot Summer Night', with soul style vocal harmonies backing Jimi's lead that hearken back to his early involvement with soul shows. It was the sort of material that did not greatly impress Jimi's hardcore English blues fans. They would have preferred more simple shuffle beat blues like 'Come On', that featured some of Hendrix' fastest licks. And there is an interesting chord section here that for a self-taught musician showed a remarkable grasp of different schools of guitar playing.

After the Robert Johnson style 'Gipsy Eyes', is a marvellous production of 'Burning Of The Midnight Lamp.' with a variety of sounds and feeling of grandeur that would have done credit to Phil Spector.

A cough and a sniff introduces the grooving blues 'Rainy day, dream away'. A strong Traffic feel is evident from the saxophone of Chris Wood and Steve Winwood's Hammond organ. Just before the fade out, Jimi starts to 'talk' through his guitar in most extraordinary fashion. Thence comes the Merman.

Here is Jimi's poetry, unfortunately elusive, no matter how hard one strains ones ears. It sounds meaningful and sincere, but Jimi's frequently slurred diction, and the deliberate distortion added to the vocal track do not help. On the extended ideas of 'Moon, turn the tides . . . gently gently away', there is much sympathetic percussion from Mitch while Jimi manages to produce the impression of wind, tides, and sea gulls from his position in the control room and behind the guitar. At the time it didn't seem to have much to do with the Experience. And of course it didn't have anything at all to do with their image. But it was a new direction, just a couple of years before its time, both for Jimi and his audience.

Amazingly funky was 'Still Raining, Still Dreaming', with more organ coming from Steve, and chattering, shattering guitar, laying right back on the beat. This inspired mood continues into 'House Burning Down', seemingly a peace offering for fans mystified by the Merman and tides. The drums march, and here one detects Mitch's occasional problem in coming out of a fill right on target, only a minor point as his drumming is generally superb throughout. The number ends with a burst of automotive fret appeal.

'All Along The Watchtower', was one of Jimi's favourite Bob Dylan songs, and it made a fine vehicle for the band to get stuck into. 'Voodoo Chile (Slight Return)' is just that, with a typical Hendrix wah-wah guitar intro that has been imitated a thousand times since. It launched a legion of groups devoted to what became known in Britain as ''eavy music", meaning a heavy emphasis on menacing riffs and brutal percussion.

There were to be no further albums, apart from Track's useful and popular *Smash Hits* compilation, until the *Band of Gypsies* was released in 1970.

In Britain less and less was heard about Hendrix, until in May 1969 the shock news came that he had been arrested at Toronto International Airport. It came at a time when all the major rock stars were being kept under surveillance. But it was still a blow when Jimi was charged with illegal possession of narcotics.

He was released on 10,000 dollars bail and was able to give his scheduled concert at the Maple Leaf Gardens. The affair was a blow to Jimi, with his memories of a sojourn in a Swedish jail the year before. The charge was to hang over him for most of the year, and the trial did not start until June 19. But on December 15, 1969, just before Christmas, he was acquitted. The jury were out for eight and a half hours but the charges of having heroin and hashish were dropped. Jimi said: 'That was the best Christmas present Toronto could ever give me.'

The Experience officially broke up in November of 1968. One of their rare British gigs that year had been at the *Melody Maker's* festival in the grounds of Woburn Abbey, where the Experience topped the bill. It was a tremendously exciting moment when Jimi returned, but as he said later: 'It was really only a jam. We hadn't played for so long.'

Alan Walsh of the *MM* asked him why there had been such a dearth of recordings since 'Axis: Bold As Love'.

Said Jimi: 'People were starting to take us for granted, abuse us. It was that what-cornflakes-for-breakfast scene. Pop slavery, really. I felt we were in danger of becoming the American version of Dave Dee, Dozy, Mick and Tich. Nothing wrong with that, but it's just not our scene. We decided we had to end that scene and get into our own thing. I was tired of the attitude of fans that they'd bought you a house and a car and now expected you to work the way they wanted you to for the rest of your life.'

'But we couldn't just say screw them, because they have their rights too, so we decided the best way was to just cool the recording scene until we were ready with something that we wanted everyone to hear. I want people to hear us, what we're doin' now and try to appreciate where we're at.'

Where they were at then was of course the *Electric Ladyland* material like 'Cross Town Traffic' and 'House Burning Down'.

'All the tracks are very personal – they're us,' said Jimi. 'It's different to what we've ever done before – and it starts with a 90-second sounding painting of the heavens. I know it's the thing people will jump on to criticise so we're putting it right at the beginning to get it over with. I don't say it's great, but it's the Experience. It has a rough, hard feel on some of the tracks.'

Jimi also explained why he spent so much time in America: 'I'm American. I want people there to see me. I also wanted to see whether we could make it back in the States. I dig Britain but I haven't really got a home anywhere. The earth's my home. I've never had a house here. I don't want to put down roots in case I get restless and want to move on. I'll only get into the house thing when

I'm certain I won't want to move on again.

'The other reason for working in the States is that we can make twenty times more money there. And there's no harm in that . . . we have to eat like everyone else. America is so large too. When you work regularly in Britain, you end up going back to the same places. That doesn't happen in America.'

Another illuminating remark Jimi made concerned America's problems. 'I just want to do what I'm doing without getting involved in racial or political matters. I know I'm lucky that I can do that . . . lots of people can't.'

But Jimi revealed that he had sent a cheque for five thousand dollars to the Martin Luther King memorial fund because he thought it was a good way to help.

At the beginning of 1968 the band were touring America extensively. In February they went from Paris to New York and San Francisco, then continued through 28 concerts, city-hopping from coast to coast, down to Texas and up to Canada. Each of the concerts was reportedly a sell-out and there was even a gang of ticket forgers operating ahead of him in New York, Texas and Arizona. It was during this trip that Jimi went back to his home town, Seattle.

'I met my family and we were happy for a change,' said Jimi. 'I enjoyed it. I went to Garfield High School, my old school where they kicked me out when I was just 16. I did a concert for the kids there. Just me. I played with the school band in the gymnasium. Only thing wrong was that it was eight in the morning. They cancelled first class to listen to me.'

Jimi was also supposed to get an award from the mayor of Seattle, but it was Lincoln's Birthday, a national holiday, and the affair was cancelled.

Jimi compared touring with the Experience to his early days with the soul shows. 'Bad pay, lousy living and getting burned — that was those days. With Little Richard, he was the guy out front and that was it. The king of rock and rhythm, that was him. And he said he was the only one allowed to be pretty . . . that was when I got a fancy shirt because I was dragged at wearing his uniform. "Take off those shirts," he told me and another guy.'

After all the hard work, it was time to take a break. Anyone who has ever witnessed a touring rock band in action will be amazed at the amount of stamina it requires to stand up to the endless routine of flights (which can be nerve wracking in themselves), concerts and hotel rooms. Eventually musicians grow heartily sick of the hotels and aeroplanes and food, and if they don't crack up and resort to drink or drugs, then they break up.

And that's what happened to the Experience. In November 1968 it was announced that the band were to go their separate ways. Said Jimi: 'Mitch and Noel want to get their own thing going — producing and managing other artists. In the New Year we'll be breaking the group apart from selected dates. Oh, I'll be around, don't worry . . . doing this and that. But there are other scenes we want to get into.'

It was at this time that 'All Along The Watchtower', from *Electric Ladyland* was a single hit in Britain. 'It's groovy, but we had no say in the choice of material that was released. But I'm glad people haven't forgotten us in Britain. We're not abandoning anyone. We're like a band of musical gypsies moving about everywhere.'

In March 1969 Jimi gave an interview in which he remarked on the pressures of the music business: 'That's the trouble with this business. People see a fast buck and have you up there being a slave to the public. They keep you at it until you are exhausted and so is the public, and then they move off to other things. That's why groups break up – they just get worn out. Musicians want to pull away after a time, or they get lost in the whirlpool.

'Mitch and Noel were quick in wanting to come back home from the States. There is all this violent thing in the States right now. It's really a clash between the new and the old. They make black and white fight against each other so they can take over at each end.

'If they can get the Black Panthers fighting the hippies – who are really the young whites – then we will all be right back where we started off twenty years ago. This is what they are trying to do. It bothers me some Black people now can't get into our music right away because they are so hung up about other things.'

Then Jimi stated: 'It's funny the way most people love the dead. Once you are dead you are made for life. You have to die before they think you are worth anything.

'And I tell you, when I die, I'm not going to have a jam session. And knowing me, I'll probably get busted at my own funeral. I shall have them playing everything I did musically, everything I enjoyed doing most. The music will be played loud and it will be *our* music. I won't have any Beatles songs, but I'll have a few of Eddie Cochran's things and a whole lot of blues. Roland Kirk will be there and I'll try and get Miles Davis along if he feels like making it. For that, it's almost worth dying, just for the funeral.'

In February 1969 Jimi played two concerts at London's Albert Hall, and already there was a new age-group of fans to see him. In the summer he made an appearance at the unique Woodstock Festival. For most of '69, however, Jimi was in exile, staying at home in New York with a few friends. Early in 1970 he unveiled the Band of Gypsies. The name came from his expression for himself and travelling friends, and featured old friends Billy Cox on bass guitar and Buddy Miles on drums.

They cut one album, 'live' at the Fillmore East in New York on New Year's day, and Miles' presence is strongly felt. Jimi plays well, and the tunes like Buddy's popular 'Changes' are good. But there is a strangely flat atmosphere difficult to define. The backing is competent and Buddy's drums had a sure-fire pulse, quite opposed to Mitch

Mitchell's more embroidered style. Tunes like 'Who Knows' that goes on for some nine minutes have little out of the ordinary to match the rivetting power of the original Experience. It was a new phase, valid in its way, but still not quite right.

At a concert in New York's Madison Square Gardens, Jimi stopped playing after a few numbers and left the stage, saying they were not getting it together.

Later that year he began working again with Mitch but retaining Billy Cox on bass. In May Jimi said: 'It was always my plan to change the bass player. Noel is definitely out. Billy has a more solid style, which suits me. I'm not saying anyone is better than the other – just that today I want a more solid style. I'm not sure how I feel about the Experience now. Maybe we could have gone on but what would have been the point of that – what would it have been good for? It's a ghost now – it's dead like back pages in a diary. I'm into new things and I want to think about tomorrow, not yesterday.'

'I wasn't too satisfied with the Band of Gypsies album. If it had been up to me, I would never have put it out. From a musician's point of view it was not a good recording and I was out of tune on a few things. Not enough preparation went into it. We owed the record company an album – they were pushing us and here it is.'

In August, 1970, Jimi returned to Britain for the third Isle of Wight festival, one of the most star-studded ever held. He flew straight in from a party held in New York to launch the Electric Lady studios which he part-owned, and was tired. Then he, Mitch and Billy Cox didn't go on until the early hours of the morning. Jimi made the effort to play well, but if he was tired the band was under-rehearsed. Later they went on a European tour, but didn't get much further than Germany and the Baltic. Billy Cox became ill and they abandoned the tour.

It must have been a depressing time for Jimi, and yet he still talked of his plans for the future. 'I've turned full circle,' he told the *Melody Maker* in September 1970. 'I'm back right where I started. I've given this era of music everything, but I still sound the same. My music's the same, and I can't think of anything new to add to it in it's present state.

'When the last American tour finished, I just wanted to go away and forget everything. I just wanted to record and see if I could write something. Then I started thinking. Thinking about the future. Thinking that this era of music, sparked off by the Beatles, had come to an end. Something new has to come and Jimi Hendrix will be there.'

'I want a big band. I don't mean three harps and 14 violins. I mean a big band full of competent musicians that I can conduct and write for. And with the music we will paint pictures of earth and space, so that the listener can be taken somewhere.

'While I was doing my vanishing act in the States I got this feeling that I was completely blown-out of England. I thought they had forgotten me over here. I'd given

them everything I'd got. I thought maybe they didn't want me anymore, because they had a nice set of bands. Maybe they were saying, "Oh we've had Hendrix, yeah he was okay." I really thought I was completely through here.

'The main thing that used to bug me was that people wanted too many visual things from me. I never wanted it to be so much of a visual thing. When I didn't do it, people thought I was being moody, but I can only freak when I really feel like doing so.

'I wanted the music to get across, so that people could just sit back and close their eyes, and know exactly what was going on, without caring a damn what we were doing while we were on stage.

'I think I'm a better guitarist than I was. I've learned a lot. But I've got to learn more about music because there's a lot in this hair of mine that's got to get out. With the bigger band I don't want to be playing as much guitar. I want other musicians to play my stuff. I want to be a good writer. I still can't figure out what direction my writing is going at the moment, but it'll find a way. I won't be doing many live gigs because I'm going to develop the sound and then put a film out with it. It's so exciting, it's going to be an audio-visual thing that you sit down and plug into and really take in through your ears and eyes. I'm so happy, it's gonna be good.'

Chas Chandler, big built, from Newcastle, a bass player with the Animals. Eric Burdon and the rest were amused when Chas wore a suit, when hair and denim was the customary garb. But he knew his future did not lie in bass playing even when the group were hitting the chart with 'We've Got To Get Out Of This Place'. The appearance of the suit was a sign that Chas was entering the Business.

But it is doubtful if Chas had any idea his first discovery would have such impact and become such an integral part of the incredible boom in rock music that was to come. In 1966 Hendrix was just a Greenwich Village jammer and Chas Chandler was quitting music, believed destined for obscurity.

In 1972, a year after the death of Hendrix, Chas was still using his energy and Newcastle shrewdness to push rock talent, managing the affairs of a successful chart band, Slade, assisted by colleagues from the Animals, John Steele and Hilton Valentine.

'It's about time somebody wrote the truth about Jimi after all that crap that has been said.' Chas explained how he came to meet Jimi, who was unknown in both Britain and America.

'I came into contact with him through Linda Keith who was Keith Richard's girlfriend. She had heard I was going into record production and told me there was a guy in the Village who was great. I met her and we went to see him working with drums and bass in the Cafe Wha in the Village. Before we saw him play, Jimi and I sat and talked. I wanted to take him back to England even before I heard him play. He was about 23 – that was in 1966 – and I was 28.

'The Animals had just started our last American tour and it was late July. Jimi didn't just say: 'Yeah man, I'll come over to England.' He was worried about the equipment we had in England and what the musicians were like. One of the first things he asked me was if I knew Eric Clapton. I said, sure I knew Eric very well and that I saw a lot of him socially at that time. He said: "If you take me to England will you take me to meet Eric?" I told him that when Eric heard him play he would be falling over to meet Jimi, and that clinched it.

'After we talked, he played. Of course he didn't do anything like the act the Experience became famous for, but there were things there we later exaggerated. He was playing the blues and he didn't do any singing. He was very hung up on his voice, and he didn't think he could sing at all.'

'In the meantime I'd found the song "Hey Joe" by Tim Rose and wanted to record it. When I saw Jimi at the cafe I never mentioned it to him, but that was the one song he actually played all night. I thought it was a kind of signpost. Incidentally, Jimi had another guitarist with him that night, Randy California, who was then 15 and later went on to join Spirit. Actually I didn't want him in the band because he was just playing down home blues and I felt with Jimi there wasn't room for another guitarist. And I saw Jimi playing in a different way.

'Jimi wasn't known at all at this time, but I hadn't any doubt in my mind. To me he was fantastic. I thought there must be a catch somewhere. Why hadn't anyone else discovered him? He was calling himself Jimmy James at the time but his real name was James Marshall Hendricks. Actually I can't remember if we changed his name from Hendricks to Hendrix, but Jimi we changed, from Jimmy. We wracked our brains trying to think of a name for the group and we didn't find The Experience until we found Mitch and Noel. Jimi had a few doubts about the name, but I said that soon it would take on a different meaning.

'I finished the tour with the Animals and the rest of the group went back to England while I stayed on in New York. We had to arrange a passport and find his birth certificate, which took a few weeks. We sat out five weeks, lurching around the Village together. He was working there backing people and I'd watch him to get ideas. I'd always been a science fiction freak and had a book which I told him to read. It was called *Earth Abides*. It really turned him on to science fiction, and that's where a lot of his lyrics come from.'

'He was still worried about coming to England though. He'd never been abroad before except with the Army. He'd been a paratrooper, and I think they flew him to Spain, dropped him out, picked him up and flew him home to New York.

'He was in the 101st Airborne and he got a medical discharge when he broke an ankle on a jump. He had volunteered as a regular when he was 17.

Chas Chandler: The Discovery of a Super-Star

'In September 1966, we arrived in England. On the 'plane he had been worrying how his American style of playing would fit with English guys, so I decided when we got to London Airport to drive to Zoot Money's, which was on the way into town. I thought if he met Zoot it would dispel his fears about English musicians.

'We arrived at Zoot's house at 11 a.m. and Jimi started jamming for two or three hours. The house was full of musicians and it made him feel he could settle in England. He took to Zoot like a fish to water. He booked into the Hyde Park Towers hotel and started to meet all the other musicians in London.

'I remember a party — it was my birthday, and we held it in Ringo's flat in Montague Square, where I had just moved in. We invited a few friends and forty people turned up. We got kicked out the next day.

'Two weeks after we arrived in England I was in our offices in Gerrard Street. A kid came in and asked if he could audition for lead guitar with the new Animals. But the place was already filled. I told him we needed a bass guitarist to work with Jimi. I lent him my bass and told him to go and meet Jimi and jam a bit to get to know him. He played bass for the first time and Jimi liked what he played. Jimi said: "I think we've found a bass player." And Noel said: "I'll switch to bass. I don't see anybody else playing lead guitar with this bloke."

'Noel was broke and I had to lend him five bob to get home. Then I heard that Mitch Mitchell had been kicked out of the Blue Flames (Georgie Fame's band). I liked his drumming and asked Mitch down. The first time all three of them got together they played non-stop for four hours.

'We went down to Blaises club where Brian Auger was playing. Jimi sat in and Johnny Halliday saw him. He asked if Jimi had an outfit because he was doing a tour of France and wanted another group. So their first appearances were on tour with Johnny Halliday. I was already fixing a deal with a record company when Kit Lambert (co-manager of the Who) saw Jimi play at the Scotch Of St. James. Kit nearly knocked all the tables over in the Scotch and wanted Jimi to be on the new label he was launching — Track. We made a deal that we would release the first record on Polydor, then join Track which was not starting up until March.

Publicity shot of the Experience, April 1967.

'After we made the first record I took it to Decca but they turned it down. The A&R man who turned it down told me: "I don't think he's got anything." The record was "Hey Joe". I took it straight over to Kit and he said: "If there's any trouble distributing I'll take it round the shops myself."

'When we came back from France, things were very quiet. It was very hard to get work and no one would touch him. I was fast running out of money. I had six guitars and I sold five of them to pay for a reception at the Bag O'Nails. I invited all the promotion men down to try and get some work.

'He played at the Bag and Phillip Hayward, who was running some clubs, asked for him for £25 as a support group to the New Animals.'

'I think the gig was at Croydon. From then on Jimi never looked back and got regular work. I went to every gig and we spent an hour discussing it afterwards. He was still working out the act that was to become famous.

'At Croydon on that first gig I think the audience were shocked. Their reaction wasn't excitement — I think they were numb! They weren't sure what it was about. Next we got a gig at the Roundhouse in Chalk Farm. Jimi got his guitar nicked and I was flat broke, so I had to sell my last guitar. I swopped my last bass for a new guitar for Jimi. Two days later "Hey Joe" hit the chart. It was all done by the skin of my teeth. The deejays hadn't been playing it on the radio, but the word had spread through the ballrooms, and it started to sell. I think we had about thirty shillings left between us.

'My fucking partner Mike Jeffery had disappeared. He hadn't even seen Jimi. He managed the Animals, and when I left them he was supposed to be my partner. I never saw the cunt again until April.' As 'Hey Joe' rocketed up the chart, Jimi began playing off some bookings at all the top London discos. 'In November he played at Blaises, and he wrote 'Purple Haze' while he was waiting to go on in the dressing room at the Upper Cut'.

Was Jimi excited by all these events?

'Excited? Yeah. But Jimi never changed, all the time I knew him. Those London club dates were fortunate because everybody came to see him including Jagger and Jones and the Beatles. They all went around telling

Hendrix at the Bag O'Nails.

43

people about the cat playing guitar with his teeth.'

It wasn't long after his first hit single that Jimi found himself involved in one of the last of the old style pop package tours that his kind of music and stage act would eventually make obsolete.

'Dick Katz was the agent. He got the tour for us and I rubbed my hands. He was on the same bill as the Walker Brothers, and I knew they were going to split up after the tour. They were supposed to be the big sex idols of the time, but we knew Jimi would cop all their reputation. So we worked on this big flamboyant sex act. One night he would do a sexy routine and the theatre managers would get on to the tour manager and tell him to clean up his act. When somebody from the circuit came round I'd whisper in Jimi's ear to cool it.'

How did the famous guitar burning episode develop on the opening night of the tour?

'We were sitting around in the dressing room trying to think of something new to put in the act. I think it was Keith Altham's idea to set fire to the guitar. Jimi had been doing a number called "Fire", and Keith said wouldn't it be great if he could start one. So we sent the roadie out to buy a tin of lighter fuel. We had to make sure it wasn't too obvious.

'I sprayed it on his guitar, but when the moment came, the matches kept going out! Jimi was lying on his back, striking matches for five minutes.

'There was a tremendous row back stage afterwards, with the theatre manager demanding the guitar for evidence.'

'For the rest of the tour they didn't take too kindly to us. John Walker was a bit of a big head and he would waltz into our dressing room and say: "I don't want any upstaging tonight. Who do you think you are?"

'There was a lot of ill feeling back stage, and they would screw up the lights, or put the house lights up on the audience during his act. It was quite a tour. There were no barriers in pop then, no pseudo hippies. It was all entertainment and a great tour for the audiences.'

Was Hendrix' 'wild man' image thus totally fabricated?

'When we saw how audiences reacted to

On Tour, 1967, with Cat Stevens, one of the Walker Brothers and Engelbert Humperdinck.

44

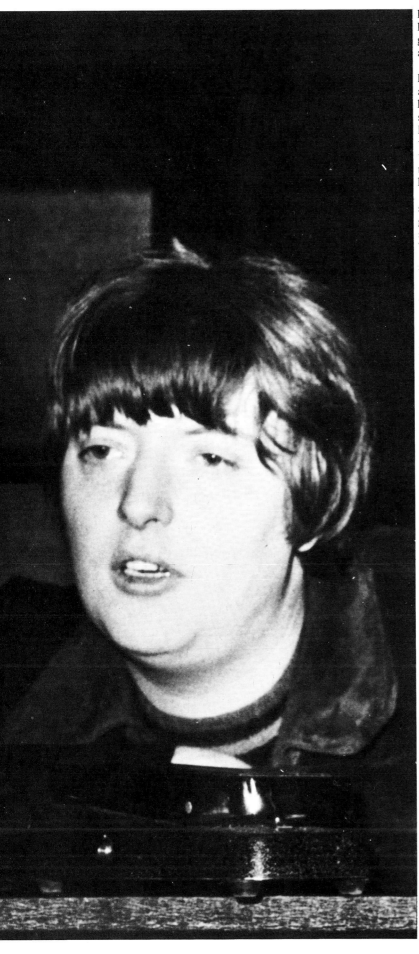

him, we followed it up. We didn't deliberately set out to do it, but when the glossy magazines picked up on him it created an incredible amount of press.'

'His ban from theatres was a bit of PR licence. We were kept informed if there was a representative of the theatre circuit in the house and we would tip Jimi off. It was the strangest mixture of people on that tour. Most of the artists got on well and Jimi used to dig Engelbert Humperdinck. He'd listen to the guy's voice and say — "he's got so much power". Jimi had no prejudice at all in his mind. He'd stand and watch a band and it could have a lousy guitarist but he would see something the guy was trying to do and go home and practise. The tour was very successful and all the concerts were sold out. The Walker Brothers were a hell of a draw. It was a break for everyone. I never bought a bass guitar again!

'Jimi had a ball, he loved it. It was then it dawned on him he could be successful and that he could do something big and lasting. It was then he got his confidence. If you didn't know him it would seem he had no lack of confidence, but he was always very nervous and I had to talk to him before every show and tell him people really did like him. The best thing was he seemed to be able to talk to the audience. Before, if an amplifier broke down on stage he wouldn't be in total control but the first night he played at the Saville Theatre in 1967 with the Who his amplifier caved in and he started talking and chatting up the audience.

The amps went wrong because of the pounding he gave his equipment. He was using feedback as an integral part of his music. The best sound he got was with Sun amplifiers in America. But after six weeks he shook them to pieces. I never saw anyone else use feedback the way he did. He'd have two strings feeding back and he'd play melody on another two while he was singing . . .'

Jimi didn't get it from Pete Townshend. The only guitarists he had heard before he came to England were Eric Clapton and Jeff Beck. He wasn't really aware of what Pete was doing with feedback because the Who hadn't really made it big in America at that time. He was into feedback, but nobody gave him credit for what he was doing so he didn't know he was doing impossible things!

'I think Jimi played the Saville (London's

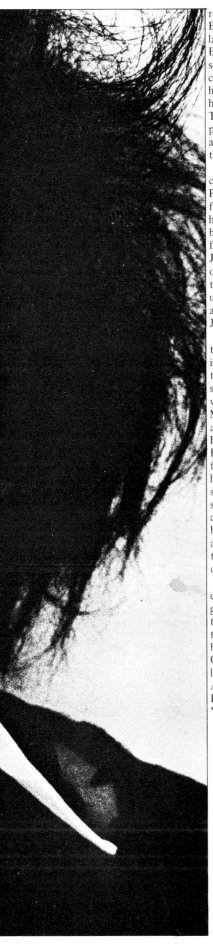

rock venue of 1967 run by the late Brian Epstein) about three or four times. On the last one, between shows, we got a call that Eppy was dead. It was an almost hysterical scene and the second house was stopped. We couldn't believe Eppy was dead. Jimi and I had been to Brian's house a few times. When he died he left a big gap on the music scene. The Saville was his plaything really, but he put on some great shows. I think he paid about £30,000 for the Four Tops and the theatre only held 1200.

'Then came Monterey. We got a 'phone call from John Phillips of the Mamas and Papas who was helping to organise the festival. Paul McCartney had been over helping him and McCartney said it wouldn't be a pop festival without Jimi. It was the first festival of its kind ever held. Brian Jones flew over specially to introduce Jimi on stage. They had met when Jimi first came to England and were good friends. They used to go to the Crazy Elephant club a lot, and Brian was one of the first to rave about Jimi.'

'We all realised something big was going to happen at Monterey. It was such a good idea and it could only have been done through the goodwill of the artists. They sent us a first class air ticket, and there we were in Monterey with Otis Redding and the Mamas and Papas and 7,000 fans in front of an enormous stage the size of the Odeon Hammersmith. They had never heard of him. But there was an air of expectancy backstage from the people who had heard the rehearsals. He went on stage and created a sensation. The first couple of numbers were slow. Then they did "Rolling Stone". The audience went berserk, we let off smoke bombs and his guitar caught fire. The Mamas and Papas had to follow him and it took thirty minutes to quieten the audience down.

'I was in the lighting box at the back during his act and it took me 25 minutes to get through the crowd backstage. When I got there, all Mike Jeffery was doing was tearing the group off a strip because they had broken a 150 dollar mike stand. But Bill Graham came over and asked us if we would like to play the Fillmore West with Jefferson Airplane. So from Monterey we went to San Francisco. Meanwhile Mike had gone to New York and he 'phoned to say he had pulled off a deal for a great American tour with the Monkees. He said the Monkees were what was happening. I hung up. We played the Fillmore and Bill Graham gave us 2,000 dollars each as a bonus when the Airplane cried off the rest of the gigs after our first night. Bill also gave us antique engraved watches. Bill has had a lot of mud slung at him, but he's a gas.'

'We went back to New York and Mike Jeffery was jumping up and down, saying he had pulled off a great deal. We all sat looking at each other. I said it would be a fucking disaster, and I wouldn't go. But Mike had signed the deal and it was too late. I told the boys I wouldn't go with them on the tour.

'They went — and died the death. I met Dick Clark who was promoting the tour and said we had to think of something — Jimi couldn't play to a bunch of 12 year olds. Dick said he would let them off the contract, so we put out a story about the Daughters Of The American Revolution waging a campaign to get him banned. But as far as we knew nobody from the Daughters Of The American Revolution had ever seen him, and most of the audience were young kids who didn't understand him anyway.

'When I told Mike what I'd done, all hell broke loose. He said I was a stupid idiot and shot off to Majorca for seven months. We never heard a word from the Daughters. I don't suppose they read the underground press. But if they did it was something they would have said anyway.

'Then Frank Barsalona came along from Premiere Talent in New York. He put on a concert in New York's Central Park with Jimi and the Young Rascals. Jimi didn't blow the Rascals off stage, but he was given a tremendous reception. We got seven more dates as a result. *Are You Experienced* went up the LP chart, and we came back to England.'

'Frank held an option for the next tour, but I found Mike had signed with another agency. I went through a four month period trying to undo all the fuck-ups. But as far as Jimi's popularity was concerned, it was like a snowball running down a hill. I'd never seen anything like it. From September '67 to July '68 he was enormous.'

What sort of changes did this bring upon Jimi?

'He started drinking quite a lot. At first

he never drank much: three whiskeys and he was happy. Jimi lived with me for two years and I would never presume to say I knew him. Nobody knew him. He never seemed to confide in anybody. But at the time there was never any sign of strain, except for his drinking. I think he was just enjoying the delights of alchohol. Eric Burdon was on his big acid scene then, but Jimi would just say, 'Oh, he's an acid freak,' and put that whole scene down. It wasn't until the time of the second album that I realised he had in fact been taking it. He'd split for a couple of days, and I realised he was on acid. At that time everybody thought it would sort out their problems. I took it eight times and was spaced out for 18 months. Half way through *Axis: Bold As Love* he was dropping it everyday. I told him he'd have to be straight some of the time. At first I thought I would give him a new slant to his lyrics, but he'd lose his temper.'

'There were so many people hanging around him, he couldn't be himself. We had an argument about it, and he said, "Okay, no more." Then someone would turn up at the studio with a bag of goodies and pour some more down his throat. Mike Jeffery turned up at the studio as well and stuck his oar in. Things began to deteriorate. And there was a big row over the cover which Mike said was a piece of crap.

'There was a dreadful atmosphere in the studio, which was full of hangers-on. We did six tracks for the Electric Ladyland album, and nobody was ready to compromise anymore. All I was doing was sitting there collecting a percentage. So I said, 'Let's call it a day.' That was late '68.

Chas ceased to be Jimi's producer and manager, but he knew what was happening. 'There were a few heavy incidents. He smashed up a place in Sweden and hit a girl in Los Angeles. He smashed up two cars in LA in one week. He went through a wierd period. He wouldn't listen to anybody. And I had no way of saying anything. He was tearing himself apart for no apparent reason. I wasn't wanted anymore, so I split and flew back to England.

'After seven months I saw him in Gothenburg, Sweden, and he asked me to take over the act again.

'I said it was a bit of an about face. But we went back to London and played at the Albert Hall. They were making a film of it and everything was so chaotic I went down to the Hall to help get it sorted out. Next day was a wierd scene. Mike wanted to do a deal. He wanted me to handle the group while Jimi went back to New York to pick up some gear and start rehearsing and recording. Then I got a 'phone call from Jimi in New York asking if there was some way we could arrange for me to become his manager. I said – no way.

I never heard any more about him for three months until two days before he died. He asked me to produce for him again. He rang me again on the Thursday and we got to discussing the design for a cover. He said he was going to America to pick up some tapes for his next album. He was happy, but he had been recording for over a year and a half and hadn't really produced anything.

Friday morning I took a train to Newcastle. When I got to the station I was met by my father who told me Jimi was dead. I couldn't believe it. I was numb for days. But somehow I wasn't surprised. I don't believe for one minute he killed himself. That was out of the question. But something had to happen and there was no way of stopping it. You just get a feeling sometimes. It was as if the last couple of years had prepared us for it. It was like the message I had been waiting for.'

Subsequently I was told that four weeks before he died he had asked a dozen people to produce for him, which left me wondering whether or not he was serious in asking me back. On the 'phone he said the only recordings of his he liked had been *Axis* and *Experienced* and that nobody could tell him whether what he was putting down was good or bad.

He had great difficulty in judging his own work. It wasn't through a lack of confidence. It was fear of lack of acceptance because his work was so personal to him. He put so much of himself into it. If a record wasn't liked it was a rejection of himself.

'It was nothing to do with colour either. I don't think he even thought about colour – it was never there. And it didn't occur to people that knew him. It wasn't until much later than an American newspaper called him a "Black Elvis". But he wasn't that either. He was somebody totally unique. He had so many things going for him, nobody noticed he was coloured.'

How close was his relationship with Mitch Mitchell and Noel Redding?

'He loved Mitch's drumming, but he didn't love Mitch. Mitch used to bug him. He got on well with Noel but used to criticise his playing. It was a love-hate relationship. Noel and Jimi in a dressing room was like a double act, with Jimi as the straight man. Noel was a strong-willed guy. If ever Jimi had an argument with Mitch, Mitch would go along with him. But Noel could always cool Jimi off. A couple of times Jimi could have murdered Noel but he never lifted a finger to hurt him.'

'The performance at the Royal Albert Hall concert wasn't the Experience that I knew. It was like three individuals on stage. Mitch was playing drum solos on every number and Jimi was playing as if there were two strangers with him. I would have said that Jimi should have gone solo, but it would have meant a lot of business hangups. It was my honest opinion that he was best with the same instrumentation. I was dead against Buddy Miles coming into the band. He was a fine rock drummer but he certainly wasn't good enough for Jimi, or Billy Cox.'

How did Jimi handle his money?

'He gave vast sums away. He gave some to his parents. And I remember once in Los Angeles he gave two girls three thousand dollars to go out shopping. He'd go out and buy nine guitars. Or he'd crack up a new Stingray, then go out to buy another and smash that up four days later. He just seemed to lose all sense of proportion. He spent unbelievable sums of money.

'In Gothenburg in January '68 he had been in a big fight at his hotel and smashed up the place. I went to the jail in Gothenburg and he was sitting in a bare cell. He had been in hospital first to have stitches put in two gashes in his hands. Then they put him in a cell. He had been absolutely out of his mind.'

'I asked him what happened, but he didn't know himself and I never really got the full story. But I think Noel hit Jimi and Jimi laid out two cops and tried to jump out of the window. He had to pay a percentage of his weekly wage, and it cost him a fortune. He also had to pay damages to the hotel. But afterwards he carried on as if it had never happened.

'When I split from them Noel had more money than the rest put together. Jimi took half and the others a quarter each. But Jimi would spend all his. He'd hire a suite of rooms at every hotel on the road, and have ten people round for steaks. Noel would stay with the roadies and save. Success never seemed to change him. He was always the same happy little guy. And yet they'd have some bitter arguments. I'll never know why — it was so hard to take Noel seriously.'

'I suppose the difference between Jimi and the group was that Mitch and Noel attached the greatest importance to gimmicks, whereas Jimi would spend time practising with his wah-wah pedal to get new sounds, Mitch wanted bigger drum kits, or Noel would want an eight string bass guitar. It's trite to say there are pressures on musicians, but there were a million on Hendrix.'

Noel Redding: 'Put It Down To Experience'

Noel David Redding, born Folkestone, Kent, December 25, 1945. Bass guitarist with Jimi Hendrix from October 1966 to July 1969. Originally a commercial artist, he turned guitarist and ended up playing bass for the most sensational act in rock.

When he left the Experience in July 1969, it was reported that 'Noel was not consulted by Jimi over his plans to extend the trio into a creative commune, which would include writers as well as more musicians.' At the time Noel had already formed his own group, Fat Mattress, which included his oldest friend, Neil Landon. The split was the first sign to the outside world that all was not well with the Experience.

How did Noel become involved in the fortunes of Hendrix?

'I was twenty. I got me guitar and went to London with ten bob in my pocket. I was going to take a job when I saw in the *Melody Maker* that Eric Burdon wanted a guitarist. I went round and played at this club called The Phone Booth. Chas Chandler was there and Eric Burdon walked past – real stars! Chas asked me who I had played with, and I said Johnny Kidd. I had – I'd once played with his guitar in a dressing room.

'Burdon had got a guitar player already, so Chas said to come down to this other audition. He asked me if I could play bass for a bit. So I went down, and there was Jimi Hendrix with a guitar. He showed me some chords, we tuned up and played. It was "Hey Joe". He bought me a drink and said he'd just come from America. Then he gave me ten bob and a bar of chocolate. I was really hungry.

'I went back the next day and Jimi surprised I had remembered the chord sequence. I don't read music, but I've got a good memory. We tried a few different drummers – me and this coon from America. Yes, that's what I used to call him. Jimi loved that – he really dug it. He loved me y'know – and I loved him.'

There were several auditions for drummers. 'I should have asked Aynsley Dunbar, shouldn't I?' said Noel wryly. 'But we got Mitch. After three days rehearsal we were playing in Paris. We knew three songs, and we had to carry our own gear. Yet we really went down so well. We couldn't believe it!'

'Back in London we did some gigs and Paul McCartney came to see us. It was fantastic. Then I found out how much money the group were earning on gigs. I was getting only £15 a week. I resigned and they put the money up to £25 a week. I resigned again and they put it up to £35. Then I resigned again and it went up to £200. I found out that in the Spring of '67 we were earning £1,000 a night – and that was a lot of money then. We split the money 50 per cent to Hendrix, 25 per cent between me and Mitch, and 25 per cent to Mike Jeffery and Chas Chandler, plus agency fees. In 1968 we were getting 70,000 dollars a night. We did one show at the Madison Square Gardens in New York for 105,000 dollars. I wish I had some of that now.'

How had Noel viewed the concept of the

Experience in the initial stages?

'I thought of us as a band and of being successful and working a lot. I thought it would be a great group, and it was. It could have been even better if we had stayed together. In 1969 I had already produced Fat Mattress's LP. Chas took over my career and said he would help me. So we did Fat Mattress just before Christmas, but it just went wrong and it should never have happened. Then all my divorce crap came up. I said I'd do a 1970 tour with Jimi and Mitch, and it was all going to be cool again. I even went early to the rehearsal. But nothing happened. I called up Mitch and he said they had already got a bass player.'

'That's when I got angry with Jimi. He wouldn't tell me himself. So I went ahead and produced an LP in the States with Lee Michaels and Roger Chapman and a 15 year old drummer. I paid for it all myself. They didn't release it. All it got us was a bad financial situation. I started drinking – and I got busted. Then I got sued for maintenance. I wished I'd never been a musician. Mind you, I had a Rolls Royce when I was 22. And four years on the road with the Experience is like ten years of life. We had some fun. When I started boozing, it wasn't just me – it was a tax bill for £97,000, and the fuzz trying to bust me. I couldn't understand why everybody was hassling me. I just wanted to play.'

'Around 1969 we were so overwhelmed by money and the glamour of being so-called pop stars, we all forgot we were people. We made mistakes, but if we had just done that last tour in 1970 together we would have made it again.

'Success came so fast, that when I look back I can see it took us over. Mike Jeffery had some good ideas. He was a creative manager. But when Jimi got busted for smack in Montreal, I had to call him up – and he was in Hawaii. What's that all about? He should have been there to help. But that's what happens with every group I've ever known. The manager always ends up better off than anybody in the group.'

How did Noel and Jimi get on musically?

'The only hang-ups were that Jimi tried to tell me what to play. I could learn the tempo and breaks, but I didn't want to be told what notes to play. I used to get really uptight. But Jimi and I had good communication. It was a shame that later on Jimi got too hung up with electronics and overdubbing. I used to get really pissed off. His music got too involved. He should have kept it simple, and it would have been perfect.

'I used to get uptight at recording sessions. I remember *Axis: Bold As Love* at Olympic Studios in London. We didn't rehearse. We'd go in and learn a song. Jimi would tell us what he needed. We'd do about four bass tracks, then drums and vocals, and rhythm guitar, and when it got to the thirty-sixth guitar over-dub I would lay down in the studio and go to sleep.'

'It got to the point once in New York when I told him he was a stupid cunt. He

The funeral:
Top: Johnny Winter
among the mourners.
Below: the coffin on its
way to the grave.

Top: the Hendrix family arrive
Below: Mitch Mitchell and Noel Redding on the right.

depended too much on himself as a writer, producer and musician. He was always trying to do it his way. There were times when I used to go to a club between sessions, pull a chick, come back, and he was still tuning his guitar. Oh, hours it took! We should have worked as a team, but it didn't work.

'Despite that the Experience was really happy. We had some great times. We just ran into a few disasters. All these people who say they knew Jimi — well it's ridiculous. All those chicks who say they knew him. He was very close to a chick he dug in Sweden. But the chick he met in Dusseldorf . . . well, he spent three days with her. They say they knew him — but they don't.

'Jimi was one of the most polite people I ever met. And he was really shy. He wasn't a very good business head, but he knew what went on. There was nothing he could do about it, especially when certain people were shoving tabs of acid down his throat. He was a good bloke. I only had one or two rows with him in four years, and that's pretty good when you've been on the road.

'Jimi was very trusting. I remember going to see him at Madison Square Gardens when he was playing with Buddy Miles and Billy Cox. Somebody gave him a tab of acid just before the show. He was completely freaked. And he freaked the audience and made a bad name for himself. That was around August or September 1970. He was rude to a girl in the audience, and used bad language on stage. But he was tripping — spaced out. Very sad that was. It was a tragedy for everybody. At one point I was thinking of suicide myself.'

'I'm not really sure about his death. I think the night before he dropped some acid. I don't know if it was an accident or suicide or murder. I was in the States and I heard that Bill Cox freaked. He was convinced somebody was trying to kill him. He wouldn't let anybody cook food for him. So Jimi cabled me to do the rest of a Swedish tour. I was going to go back and do the dates with him. I heard Jimi had played the Isle of Wight and wasn't all that good. The next thing I heard — he was dead.

'Mitch and me were there — at the funeral. And an American funeral ain't like they are over here. They had his body laid out in a coffin, and we had to walk past it and look. I thought we wouldn't have to — but we did. I couldn't look. Mitch and I were both crying and held hands. It was the one thing I felt really bad about. He had been dead for two weeks. The preacher should have just said: "He played great guitar, and now he's dead." But he didn't. He had to make a long solo.

'After Jimi died I couldn't talk about him to anyone, but now it's cool. He was the first close person I had known to die, and I was very upset. Now when people ask me about him I can talk because I have the feeling he is around somewhere. He's probably forming a band right now with Buddy Holly and Eddie Cochran. They should have buried his white Fender guitar with him. It was his favourite.'

Jeanette Jacobs:'He Said He'd Buy Me Everything'

Jeanette Jacobs was a friend of Jimi's from his early days in New York. A singer, she worked with Dr. John, Cake, and Ginger Baker's Airforce. Jeanette suffered a nervous breakdown shortly after Jimi's death, and only began singing again with Maggie Bell and Stone the Crows well over a year later.

Strangely, Jeanette has many of Jimi's mannerisms, and she reminds people of Jimi in the way she sometimes sits or talks. She recalls: 'When I met Jimi all he had was two pairs of pants, two shirts and a guitar. That's all he owned. But he had a premonition about being a star. "I'm going to be very big," he once said, and that was before he met Chas. He said to me: "You're going to have all the clothes you want when I'm a big star." He'd take down the addresses of clothes shops, and say: "You can have this, and that . . ."

'We used to go around together in New York and LA. It was off and on. He was a very sensitive person and that shyness was real. Lots of people say he put it on, but he didn't. And he wasn't at all stupid. He played stupid, but that was one of his games to see how far people would go in taking advantage of him. People would call him on the 'phone and I would be sitting there looking at him and laughing. He'd say: "I'm falling asleep . . . uh, uh, uh." Then the 'phone would drop, and he'd sit there laughing! He'd hang up and you'd hear the party saying "Hello, hello?" Actually, I think he would have been a good actor.'

'I remember when I was on tour with him and he blew a concert. This was in New York City. He said he was too tired and sick and they called it "exhaustion". After he put the 'phone down, he watched TV for a time. Then he said: "Let's go out to a place where nobody will see us," and we ended up at the Scene Club. The roadie saw us and said: "I thought you were supposed to be sick." Jimi said: "You can get well you know. There's no time limit."

'I think because of his mother's death, he didn't have a happy childhood. That really stayed in his head all the time. He used to grab drinks out of my hand and say, "You've had enough." His mother used to drink, and he'd say: "Please don't drink, you're the only girl who could make me cry apart from my mother."

'He was very lonely. That's what he says in his songs, like "The Wind Cries Mary". Other bands would say to me, "I bet you don't know he beats up girls and puts them in hospital." They didn't know I knew him, and I'd say: "Maybe the girls made him uptight." I used to make him uptight sometimes. But all he did was ignore me for a day. He was a big games player.

'Once he tried to fake a suicide. He took two sleeping pills. He thought I had gone out with one of the band and he got jealous. When I came into the room he was all done up and in the middle of his so-called delerium. He got up, though, and said: "Did you ball?" Very straight. And I said "No!" He was just playing, and I said that was great acting.

'In his life he loved four girls. I was one, Fay was another – a girl he went out with when he was 16. And Cathy Etchingham. And then there was Monika Danneman, but she was a bit of an escape for him. He really needed a home and an old lady. We all need that one special thing – I mean "Cry of Love."

'His death was the combination of a lot of things. He'd taken quite a few drugs in his life. The name of his group was him. He experienced everything he could. Jumping from aeroplanes, that's a rush in itself. Smashing a window with his hand. He got me to do that too. It's a release of emotion, like screaming at the top of your lungs. Jimi wasn't really weak. He could just be swayed. And being sensitive, he was frightened some people might get hurt.'

He would say to me: "What do you want?" And I would say: "What do you mean?" And he'd say, "In the next room, you can get anything for free." I asked who they were, and he said they were fans trying to get him stoned. Not to hurt him, but to turn him on. There was anything you could think of – uppers, downers, white lightening, purple hearts, take your pick.'

'You wouldn't believe it. They really thought he could take it all at once. It's a drag to think that the people who loved him could have killed him. Not intentionally of course. He was an idol, maybe a genius, and they thought he could take everything. He enjoyed experimenting, but I never saw him take anything except acid. I know he snorted, 'cos everybody snorts something. I've never seen a needle on Jimi.

'Just before he died, Monika Danneman came and said she was madly in love with Jimi and had this ring and they were going to get married. I fell for it unfortunately and left the country. Jimi said: "Please wait." But having heard this from the girl right in front of me, I didn't have a leg to stand on. The night before he died somebody told him I had gone away. In the morning he was found dead. I just think it had to happen.

OF SUPPORTERS SIGNALLING
EVELAS HIS RELIEF **AND**
CHARGES OF DRUG POSSESSION
USED TO GIVE THEIR NAMES.UP!

*Left: after the Toronto
heroin bust, with
Jeanette Jacobs on the
right.
Below: Hendrix with
Cathy Etchingham,
January 1969, when
they lived together in
London.*

'A lot of people said that after 1968 he
was going down and down. But *Cry of Love*
doesn't sound to me like going down. To
me, that was one of his best albums. He
went through a bad time because he couldn't
get the sound he wanted. It bothered him,
but he didn't burn himself out. People just
expected Jimi Hendrix to be powerful all the
time, and he told me he got tired of doing
this physical thing. He'd do it sometimes
because they expected it, that's what they
wanted.'

'I had a nervous breakdown about two
months after he died, when I finally realised
he wasn't coming back. People say he's still
here. But mentally and physically he isn't
here. That's why he said: "When I die, just
keep playing the records." '

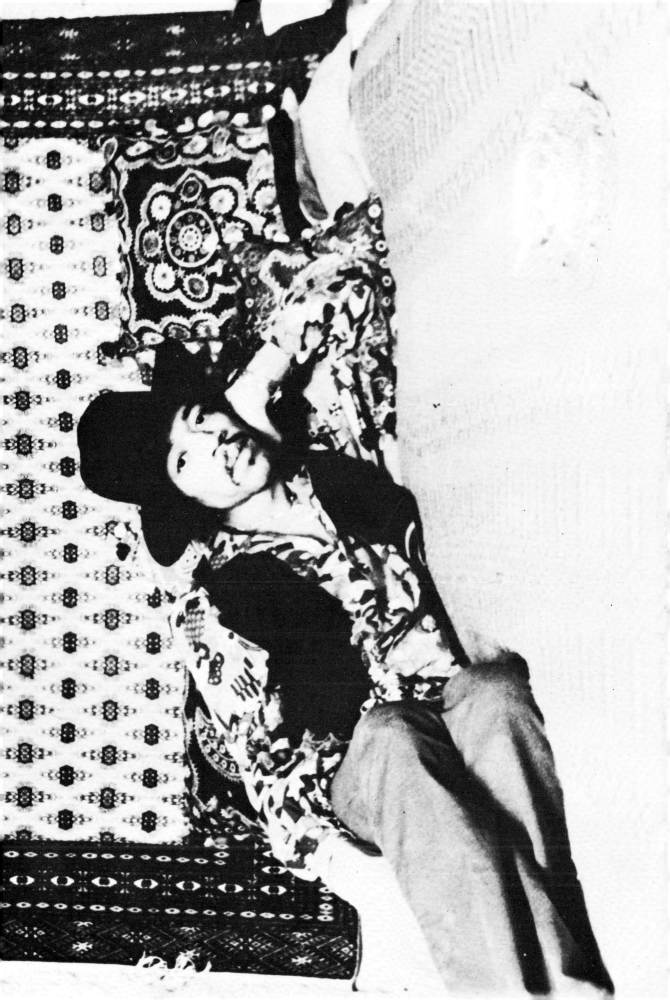

Gerry Stickells, Mitch Mitchell, Noel Redding, a friend, Hendrix and a friend at the Sgt Pepper Club.

Life On The Road: Gerry Stickells

Road managers are vital elements in the chemistry of rock. Musicians rely on them almost as much as their instrument. The good roadie has to be a combination of engineer, labourer, nurse, butler, chauffeur, bodyguard and psychologist. He might have to withstand being sworn at and even kicked, yet he can muster a dog-like devotion not seen since feudal times.

The road managers who could stand the pace and tantrums of the Jimi Hendrix Experience were indeed experienced men. They had to cope with one of the first 'heavy bands', that spent thousands on amplification and treated it with shattering contempt. If valves did not blow through the sheer force of Jimi's playing, then the speaker cabinets would be sent tumbling in the mayhem of a destructive finale. It was the roadies' job to keep the battered equipment working at all costs, and keep the powerline of communication open between

their master and his audience.

Not many could stand the strain of working for the Hendrix camp. A tough young Scot, who took no nonsense but grew to love Jimi, stayed with him right to the end. Eric Barrett, from Glasgow, was employed by Gerry Stickells. The latter mostly took care of business on the road, while Eric was the man on stage.

To them, the years on the road with the Experience are already a blur. They find dates hard to remember. Which chick in LA? Where did the truck breakdown? Who stole all the equipment? They are left with memories of a time they will never forget if only as a period of intense excitement

Gerry Stickells and Eric Barrett cossetted Jimi, Mitch and Noel through five years of madness. Now Stickells works at New York's Electric Lady studios, once part-owned by Jimi, while Barrett has been working for singers James Taylor and Cat Stevens.

Gerry Stickells was Jimi's road manager and personal assistant from the formation of the Experience right up to the end. He took care of business, and freely admits that he did not particularly care for the music. 'I just don't like loud rock and roll,' he says. But he resents suggestions that Hendrix was ever neglected, and rejects the climate of blame that developed after Jimi's death.

Gerry came into the Experience through the auspices of Noel Redding: 'I never really used to work for anybody before — I just used to kick around with odd bands. Noel comes from the same place as me and I knew him. He got me the job really, when he went to London to get a job with Eric Burdon and ended up playing bass with Jimi. Their first gig was in Paris with Johnny Halliday, and I joined up when they came back.

'Everything started moving along so quickly, and I was learning with them. When we first played, it was all too loud for clubs

— there just wasn't that kind of loud music around at the time.

'Jimi was an easy guy to get along with — a lot easier than he was at the end, obviously. He was easy to work with in those days because he wanted to get on. He was very keen, and he seemed to know what he wanted. Maybe the management helped make his ideas a little more practical, but he knew what he wanted from the group.

'At rehearsals, Jimi said we'll do this, this and this, and that was basically it. It was all pretty friendly — apart from Mitch who could never be on time! But there again he was famous for that.

'When we started it was a rush through all the £18 and £20 a night gigs around the country. When we went into America, it was a whole new thing again. It only lagged in the months before they broke up, when they got fed up with each other.'

Did the music go stale on Jimi?

'Well I think it was what happens with most groups – they really got fed up with what the public wanted to hear. They were working very hard, two shows a day, and had done some very hard tours of the States. We did 47 cities in 54 days on one tour. They must have got fed-up. The biggest hang-up Jimi had was getting away from his show bit, smashing up guitars, and just getting down to playing. But it was difficult to bring the public round to that. It was expected that he would set his guitar alight or smash the amplifier. He wanted to change that. But I suppose it was always in the back of his mind that if the show didn't go well, he could always win 'em over, and they would say it was a great show if he turned round and smashed up the amps. Which was an awkward position to be in.'

'After the group broke up, he didn't do anything for quite a while. He messed around with new groups, but he was never really happy with them. I think what seemed to happen to him at that period and probably towards the end of the Experience was that he became frustrated and seemed to have run out of ideas with his writing. He was always playing the guitar – but he seemed to me to be trying to get into something else. On the last album, *The Cry Of Love* he had just broken through again into writing stuff that he was happy with. He went through a bad period when he was unhappy, he couldn't seem to play or write anything that he was satisfied with. The stuff he was trying to write with his home tape recorder sounded too much like his old stuff, and he knew it himself. It was a very frustrating period for him.

'The last gig they did was the Stadium in Denver in about August or September '69. I remember the gig because we got teargassed and mobbed, and we had to lock him in the back of the equipment truck to get him out. The stage was on the football pitch, and there were about thirty to forty thousand kids and security wasn't very good. There was a police line firing tear gas shells into the audience to calm them down! Of course all the tear gas was blowing back on us.

'But then the kids just broke through the front and there was nothing to stop them, they just ran across the football pitch and all around the stage, there was no other barrier. So we just had to back up the equipment truck, lock the group in the back, and drive out through these kids. It was murder, but there was no other way out, and they squashed the roof of the truck flat. It was ridiculous.'

Apart from the problems of being a showman, what else frustrated Jimi?

'Well he was frustrated by a lot of people around him, because he wasn't the kind of person who would ever tell anybody to fuck off. He wouldn't do it, even if someone was

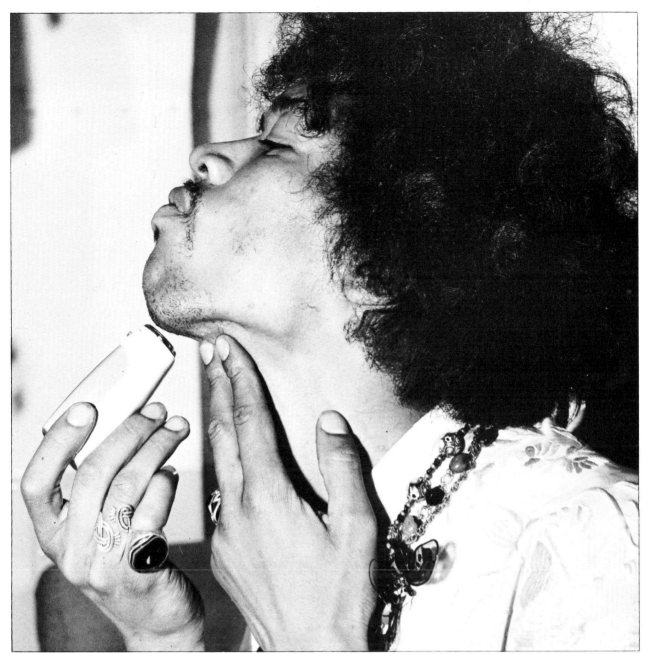

making him really uptight. Occasionally he'd tell us to do it, which we would. But then I got into the habit of throwing people out anyway, offhand, and he would say: "No – let them stay!"'

How did money affect him and how much was earned?

'Most of the shows, when he got bigger, we did on self-promotion. He was earning anything from 18,000 to 60,000 dollars a night. At Devonshire Downs, in the States, we got 100,000 dollars for 45 minutes, plus a percentage which we never got. There was a lot of chaos. That was the year that more or less killed pop festivals in America.

Did Jimi seem concerned about colour?

'To me Jimi wasn't a black man – he was a white man. He didn't think like a coloured guy, and he certainly didn't appeal to a coloured audience at all. He wasn't playing coloured music. Not that he wasn't sympathetic to their cause. He just didn't really

think about it. You could make jokes with him about it.'

Was that because of his background, or his having been in the army?

'It wouldn't be the army, because there was still a lot of prejudice in the army at that time. Maybe it was his school, and because his mother wasn't a Negro, she was an American Indian. And his father was a very easy going guy, and his step-mother was Japanese, so he didn't really think black at all.

'His father was a landscape gardener – he's retired now. His parents didn't really know what Jimi was. They knew he was a star, but being older people they weren't really into his music. When he first came out of the army he didn't go home, he started playing on the road with different people. So he hadn't been back for quite a while when we played Seattle. Half the town turned out to be his family, and crowded

backstage.

'The Mayor of the town came to his funeral. I was in London for the autopsy, and I flew the body back to Seattle. The funeral was an anti-climax really. A lot of people came because it was a place to be seen. It's hard to say how many were there. I counted about 25 limousines. There were quite a few artists, John Hammond Jnr., Buddy Miles, and a lot of promotors. The best bit I think Jimi would have enjoyed was when we rented a hall, got a few instruments and the musicians got up and jammed. We had a good party. It was the way he would have wanted. We gave him a good·send off.'

Did he have many close friends?

'No, I don't think he did have close friends. To everybody, he had a different side. I don't think anybody knew him. I knew one side of him. I don't believe anybody really knew where Jimi was at, or what he was thinking about at any point,

Hendrix, Mitchell and Redding with disc jockey Emperor Roskoe and the Duke of Bedford's son inside Woburn Abbey during the 1968 Woburn Pop Festival.

although a lot of people profess they did.

'He was never short of women, but I don't think there was anybody serious. Sometimes he used to have one girl friend for quite a while, but there wasn't one you could definitely call his old lady, and say this was the one. There was of course Devon, hanging around, God rest her soul. She O.D.'d a few months ago in New York. She was making a movie about being a junkie and going through withdrawal, and she O.D.'d while they were making the movie. Devon Wilson had been on the groupie scene for years, and like he used to hang around with her a bit.

'Before he died I'd never met this other chick, Monika Danneman. She'd been around because Eric had met her before, but in my opinion she blows it up a lot bigger than what it was.'

'I was a friend — he knew I wasn't over-enthusiastic about his music, but that

66

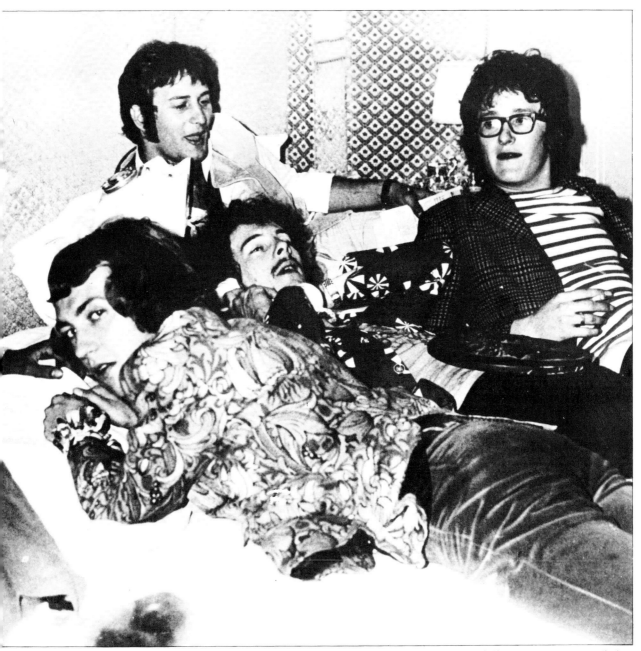

didn't stop us being friends. I'm not a great fan of loud rock and roll music. But it wasn't a thing between us — we used to laugh and joke about it. I was a friend — but I never really knew what he was thinking about.

'He had a great sense of humour, and I used to find the best times were when we were travelling alone. Outside of music, I don't think he had any real interests. Sometimes just sitting on the 'plane, he asked me about something he read in the papers, things he didn't normally think about. He was never a person to get into a political thing. A lot of people would have liked to use his name, to push their political things along. He was asked to go to the White House to see Nixon for a youth telethon. But it didn't come off, and he wasn't going to go anyway.

'Towards the end, when he became big, a lot of the black power movements tried to move him in their direction, but his heart was never in it.'

How did he get on with management?

'Pretty well in general I suppose. No rock artist ever gets on that well with his manager. Either side is always bitching about something. Jimi didn't come around to the office unless he wanted some money or some studio time. That's where he used to spend all his time — he was happy once he was in a recording studio.'

'I think he enjoyed a show but it was a case of getting him on stage. To him it was much easier going into a recording studio. But he'd be a lot happier if he'd done a show. It was just a case of getting him to go on stage and do it. Once he was out there he was fine. When there's that much money and people involved, you just can't say you don't want to do a show. The audience is waiting. The only other problem was getting them up in the morning. They'd say "Are the other two up yet? I'm not getting up until they are." And you'd go round all three of them and start lying, "Yes, the other two are down in the hotel lobby." Mitch was the worst in the world for getting up in the morning. In the States we've had to break hotel doors open and cut the chains. He'd cover the telephone with pillows so he couldn't hear anything."

How did Gerry look back on his years with the Experience?

'I think we had more good times than bad times, especially when we first started, in the days of the tour with Cat Stevens, Engelbert Humperdinck and the Walker Brothers. A more unlikely combination you couldn't imagine! It was a funny night when Jimi first set fire to his guitar. You should have seen Tito Burn's face when it went up in flames. It was at the old Astoria in Finsbury Park, London. The compere ran on to help put it out, and got his hand burnt. The funny thing

was the can of fluid was down in the pit. And afterwards when they investigated and tried to find out what was going on, I was clearing away microphones, and they couldn't see the can of fluid down in the orchestra pit where Jimi had tossed it away.

Then there's the story – just after the Cream broke up, we were doing the Lulu show on television, which was going out live. And Jimi dedicated a number to the Cream and played to the end of the show so Lulu didn't get a chance to put her last number in. The producer was tearing his hair out. There was nothing they could do!'

'And then it was funny going to Monterey pop festival, because it was like starting all over again. Jimi had reached very big in England with a couple of hits. And when we went to the States it was like being treated like a support band. But he went down very well and it was quite a shock for everybody. The record made then is worth listening to because it showed just how tight the band was. It was never as tight after that because the band never used to rehearse, and I think they got fed up with playing the same songs over and over again.'

Did Jimi's lyrics have much meaning for Gerry?

'I didn't really get into his lyrics. I took care of the business side. He used to write a lot. I'd see him on the 'plane jotting something down. I don't think he had much trouble writing though. He'd record the track in the studio first, then write the words while the rest of the group took a break for an hour.

What were his outside musical influences?

'I remember he used to listen to Muddy Waters a lot and the blues. His record collection was mostly blues, stuff I had never heard of he had got in the States.'

What albums are there left to come out of Electric Ladyland?

'It's a long process of editing and mixing what's left, because there are over 200 boxes of tapes. A lot of it you have to listen to pick out odd pieces and make things, which takes a lot of time. There won't be much more after this. We consider we have taken the best stuff. But if somebody wants to release an album of jams, there is nothing we can do about it. Our next album will be called "War Heroes".'

What had been Jimi's plans, just before he died? What was scheduled to happen next?

'Well, he was just going to start a German tour. And the *Cry Of Love* would have been released, much as it is now. I think he would have gone more into the *Cry Of Love* things. When he first started recording he had so many tunes and so much he wanted to get down, it was all stored in his head. And it seemed like that again with *Cry Of Love*. He had been frustrated for so long, and he had a new flood of ideas.'

Life On The Road: Eric Barrett

Eric Barrett had been working with the Nice in England before joining the Experience and touring the States and Europe. 'I only want to say good about Jimi,' said Eric, who now lives in Los Angeles and works for James Taylor, Tony Joe White and Cat Stevens.

'I first met Jimi when I was working at the Saville Theatre with the Koobas. They were on the same show together. He seemed like a great guy to work for, although sure as hell it wasn't my ambition. But one night, after the Speakeasy had burnt down, I was in Blaises. Noel Redding came over and said: "I've been looking for you. Our roadie has freaked out in the States. We're going to Milan tomorrow. Do you want the job?" I said we would talk about it later.

'I got home drunk at 4.30 a.m. Gerry Stickells rang at 7.30 a.m. and said: "Do you want to go to Milan?" I got up with a terrible hangover and went to the office. We caught the 'plane to Italy and they played at the Piper Club.

'This was back in '68. The equipment was in pieces because they had just finished a tour. After every number Jimi would scream at me. The amplifier tubes were shot and the power kept rising and falling all the time. Jimi kept screaming: "What's wrong?" I said, "I don't know. I'm leaving!" '

'But Gerry told me it was cool. I said the equipment was no good, and Jimi apologised and said he didn't mean to shout at me. After five days in Italy I loved him, and realised what he was trying to do.

'We had to re-build the equipment. A guy from Long Island called Tony Francis, who was a genius with amplifiers built 'em up for us. I explained the problem, that Jimi played everything at number ten on the knob — bass, treble, everything. I said the amplifiers were not lasting more than one show, and they just burnt out.

'Tony stripped it all down and built 'em up. He cranked everything up and one afternoon at a soundcheck Jimi tried it out. It worked.

'We tried Sun amplifiers, and Jimi just burnt them out. So we stuck with Marshalls. Jimi always used them, although Noel loved Sun for his bass.

'Jimi started out with 75 watts and ended up with six four by twelve Marshall cabinets, a four by twelve monitor, and four 100 watt Marshall tops, all souped-up and coupled-up through fuzz, wah-wah pedals and a Univibe! He had a special box of gadgets and the fuzz and wah-wah pedals acted as pre-amps.

'If I tried to test his equipment, all I got was feedback. Jimi could control it all with his fingers, and I still don't understand to this day how he did it. It was all part of his genius.'

'We carried two dozen fuzz boxes and two dozen wah-wah pedals. We had so many spare parts — 13 guitars, and pieces of guitar that he had smashed. He would smash a brand new guitar — it didn't matter. He loved his guitars, and the older ones were never smashed. He enjoyed smashing guitars — it got his frustrations out and the kids went beserk. I really think he enjoyed it. Out of all the bits I'd build another guitar, and he'd go out and smash it again.

'He always used a black Gibson Flying Arrow or a Gibson Les Paul for the blues. I've got his guitar and would never sell it, even if I was starving. The black Gibson has three big gold pick ups and was made for him left-handed. He used to re-string a right handed guitar left handed, and all the controls would be at the top. He couldn't play a left-handed guitar because the controls would be at the bottom.'

How did Eric explain the 'downer' period for Jimi that set in after their early successes?

'He might have been drying up with his material. He was the king guitar player. How would you feel if you were king and drying up? As soon as he got some new ideas he was so happy.

'One morning in Los Angeles — this was just before he got busted in Toronto — he called me up at midnight and told me about these great ideas. He said: "We'll only do two shows a week, and take a big top — like a circus — and we'll have it set up in the middle of a field. It'll hold a lot of people, but we won't charge them too much, and we'll use our own security so there won't be any police hassles".'

'A guy had designed the stage, which

would revolve and have lifts. The stage would be like a TV set, with everybody sitting on couches as part of the set. he really wanted to do it, and I listened to him until 9.30 a.m. – his ideas were so interesting. Two weeks later he was busted in Toronto for heroin and was completely upset. He thought he'd go down for ten years, and it wasn't even his smack. Some chick had thrown it in his bag. He wasn't feeling well when he left to go to the airport. He said he had a headache and the chick said: "This will help the headache." He never checked his bag.

'All the years I was with him I never saw a needle at anytime. Sure he smoked pot, or he'd take an upper. But he wasn't a junkie. I never saw him do anything serious. At times he was taking acid, but it wasn't like a daily event. That phase passed in everybody's lives and went as quickly as it came. Yeah, acid might have changed his personality. I don't know – I've always been a boozer.

'He was very worried by the bust and didn't do anything for a long time. Gerry was with him when he got arrested. I had driven up to Toronto and saw everybody looking as if there had been a 'plane crash. Then they told me what had happened. But he got off and was completely cleared. He threw a press conference afterwards and said: "From now on it's all uphill. I'm going to go and play for the kids".'

'After that he did Woodstock, and got a six piece together with Mitch on drums, Billy Cox on bass and a conga player – Juma. They did Woodstock and a club in New York but he realised it was not the right formula. The other guys were just jamming, and not playing properly.

'Buddy Miles was before Woodstock. They did three shows with the Band of Gypsies and they made an album. The only reports I had was that the organisation couldn't carry it. They played on the Johnny Carson TV show, Jimi's amplifier blew up and he walked off stage.'

Why did Jimi try the Band of Gypsies experiment?

'There was a point where Jimi got into Black Power and a lot of people were trying to turn him on to a heavy Black Power thing

– but it didn't last long. They told him he should work with his soul brothers, so he tried it. But I think Buddy Miles and Jimi were both front line men. Buddy played guitar as well as drums and there was a personality clash that made the band impossible.

'In 1970 we flew to the Isle of Wight. The night before Jimi and I had been to the opening of the Electric Ladyland studios in New York. We were still drunk after leaving the reception, and the hostess woke us up – in London. He hadn't played England for two years. The press were all there to meet us, and he was very happy. Two weeks later he died.

'He had wanted to do so many things. All his plans were so creative. *Cry Of Love* was recorded, he had his own studio and he wanted to get back to more recordings.

'His one big problem was that if he wanted to play anything new the kids shouted for "Hey Joe" or "Fire". He'd get really mad at that and say: "I'm not a juke box!" If he tried to give them something new, they weren't ready for it, so he wanted product [albums] out first. Then they would know the new numbers.

'I never really saw any changes in him during the time I knew him, except that he looked healthier. He looked much slimmer. If you remember the period of Lord Kitchener's Valet, his face was all broken out. But all that stuff about his hair falling out was a load of shit. He just had his hair short, for a change.

'The way I remember Jimi was that he always wanted people to share everything with everybody. He'd always introduce people to each other, and he always wanted the other guys in the band to get as much publicity as he could. He was never selfish. The only people who really knew him well were Mitch, Noel, Stickells and a few chicks.

'His favourite bands were Chicago – he loved Terry their guitarist – and the Zeppelin and Cream. He played their albums a lot. His hero was Bob Dylan. I don't know if he ever met him. But he was his hero, and he did "All Along The Watchtower". He could never remember the words – he used to sing the first verse, four times.'

An ex-*Daily Express* reporter, Robin Turner, turned PR man, was closely associated with all the top rock musicians. Although he never worked with Jimi he knew him socially, and had a newspaperman's perception of his character and problems.

'Women were one of Jimi's pleasures,' says Robin. 'He was a very erotic man and had many girlfriends, but there were few that were really close or meant anything to him. Although they all claim that Jimi wrote "Little Wing" for them, I think he just wrote it for everybody. To my knowledge Cathy Etchingham was the only girl he had any real relationship with, and he certainly got through a lot of ladies. He lived with Cathy in a flat in Brook Street for about three years. It was above a restaurant called Mr. Love. The flat had a plaque outside which said that Handel used to live there. Cathy later married Eric Clapton's chauffeur. I think Cathy met Jimi the second day he came to Britain, and they lived together –

off and on – for three and a half years.'

'There were other girls, but by the time Cathy had faded out he was past the stage of having one chick. He wanted just anybody – for company. He once said to me that he didn't like multiple scenes with girls. And yet he had them in great numbers. He was hugely insecure. He told hair-raising stories of lost money. I suppose he was prone to exaggerate, but then he was larger than life all round.

'Yes, he did care about money. He claimed that there was money that had been lost or never seen. But as everybody knows, pop stars never get into their own business.

'I think the saddest part about the funeral, and the bit that really pissed me off, was that he was buried in America. He expressly said that he wanted to be buried by the Thames, in England. He actually said "If I go – don't bury me in Seattle, it's too cold and damp there." He liked England and he didn't like Seattle. And he didn't want

people to be mournful at his funeral. He wanted them to put on all his old clothes and dance on his grave. But at the funeral it was thought that would be undignified.

'He talked about death quite a lot. He celebrated living, but he didn't expect to get old. I saw him socially quite a lot during a period when he wanted to change managers. He didn't trust anybody towards the end. Not a soul in the world. He didn't really trust Mike Jeffery but to him it was a case of "the devil you know, to the devil you don't". He was a very mixed up guy.'

'He really worked his balls off in America before he came to Britain. He was playing bass guitar and sleeping on floors, but he was never worried about money. It wasn't until he got a lot of money that he started to worry. His biggest expenditure was on drugs. He was heavily into drugs around '69 and '70. He spent a lot of time smacked-out, locked away in a flat in New York. His hair started to fall out in patches. Then he

Robin Turner: A Pressman's Eye-view

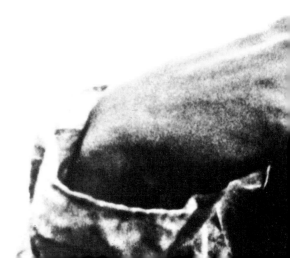

resurfaced looking gaunt and grey rather than black. He used to sit in the Speakeasy wiggling his tongue in a rude manner at passing chicks. But for a long time he vanished. No one could find him.

'He snorted heroin, which is a fairly wasteful method. But towards the end he only took small amounts. I think he was coming together, and if he had stayed around he would have made it. He was an incredible blues guitarist. He really hated what he put over on stage, but was persuaded to do that act by Chas Chandler and Mike Jeffery. And he was tied to it forever. He didn't want to seduce his guitar on stage. He was driving a runaway train and didn't really know how to stop it. I always felt he was down, even during his more violent excesses in the Speakeasy. He got caught up in the part of playing Jimi Hendrix. But I think he must have believed it. He would talk about it in a cynical way, but he believed it when he wanted to make a lot of money. Later he realised it was a difficult road back. I always remember the Lulu Show on TV when he started playing "Hey Joe", and then said, "That's enough" and played "Sunshine of Your Love", as a tribute to Ginger, Jack and Eric.'

'He did have periods of violence. There was a story about him throwing a brick at a girl in LA. Other times he was quiet and polite, and he couldn't understand why he had done something. But he did it. He was frightening in a way, because you never knew which Jimi Hendrix you were talking to, or whether you were really communicating. I felt it was always an act. I don't think there was a person in the world he trusted, but Eric Barrett and Gerry Stickells were closest to him.

'Eric Clapton and he had a strange relationship. They had a tremendous love for each other although they didn't see each other often. Clapton cried for three days after his death. He said, "How can he go, and leave me?" He saw it as Robert Johnson all over again. Eric wanted to do a Robert Johnson — a few good years and then go. When Jimi actually did that he related so much more.

'Jimi and Eric played together at Island studios when they were both doing things on Steve Stills' album. Jack Bruce came down as well. Jack and Jimi had been thinking of forming a group. And one time there was a plan to form Emerson, Lake, Palmer and Hendrix. He actually had a few plays with them.

'Jimi got used and screwed but he wanted to have success. Then he couldn't get out of it, and became cynical and distrustful. He wasn't a fool. In other circumstances I could imagine him settling down as a bank clerk — he was quietly spoken and articulate. That was the life style he may have preferred, but he was caught up. He really was an incredible guitarist. We shall not see the like of him again.'

Hendrix last concert – the Isle of Wight, 1970.

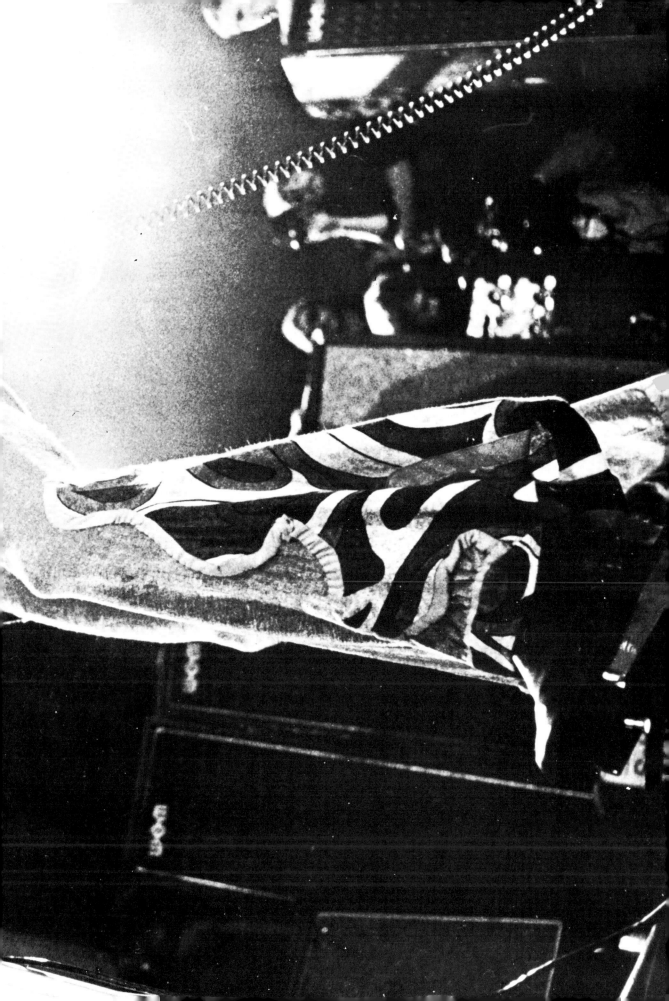

Hendrix The Musician: Bold As Love

With the development of modern systems, Jimi had more power and a greater variety of sounds and effects at his finger tips than any musician before him. Not even the electric organ can equal the range of tones and colours produced by an amplified guitar. Few instruments can reflect human emotions so directly. And while there might have been many more skilled guitar virtuosos in the world, none could equal that combination of qualities that made Jimi's style unique.

'Jimi's playing was liquid' said John Hammond Jnr. It was also fast and fluent. It could evoke violence or delicacy or create a pastiche of surrealism. He was all things to all audiences. To the jazz fan he was an embryo jazz musician. Blues fans saw him as a great new blues artist.

Guitarist and singer Johnny Winter said of him: 'He had fantastic musical ability and could create feelings nobody else could. His guitar was like an extension of his soul. It wasn't even a guitar or notes or music. It was him. He was just projecting Jimi Hendrix.'

When a great talent dies early, it is often said that perhaps it was just as well, as the talent was obviously on its way down, and that a lifetime of mediocrity lay ahead. But there is no reason to suppose that because, say, Charlie Christian died young after making a few revolutionary electric guitar records with Benny Goodman and later the pioneers of Bebop, he had passed his musical peak. Christian could have been poised on the brink of his musical fulfillment, and the same may well have been true of Hendrix.

Jimi had his battles with the guitar, and as his moods ranged in mercurial fashion, so did the quality of the music. From the tenderness of 'The Wind Cries Mary' he could beat a path to destruction and

The Record Plant, September 1968

cynicism as displayed on his dismemberment of 'The Star Spangled Banner' at Woodstock. At times he was in total command, with an endless flow of ideas pouring forth. On other occasions he seemed to be hitting brick walls that made a mockery of his style and technique. At his worst, Jimi could be flat, listless and dull. Such a disappointment was evident in his Royal Albert Hall concert in early 1969. In the process of shaking down his old image he seemed bereft of ideas. Jamming on the Cream's over-familiar 'Sunshine Of Your Love' he was playing more out of desperation than with any definite aim. But Jimi was usually seen by the public and the critics at important concerts when he was either emotionally upset or just tired and over-worked.

There is no doubt that his technical proficiency soared to new heights towards

the end of his career. From the evidence of the *War Heroes* album, released after his death, his guitar playing took on a new maturity amounting to a Hendrix renaissance. And there was once again a tremendous joy and spirit to his playing. His earlier shock tactics were giving way to the satisfaction of a mellow phrase cleanly played, a run that twisted and spiralled with devious logic, a subtle change of tone and chord to embellish and uplift an idea.

From the beginning, his 'pretty' guitar playing was never prissy, nor were his outbursts of violence vulgar. At his best Jimi could evoke that tingling sensation of the natural creative artist unleashed, offering the delights of unfettered freedom of expression, a freedom so often abused by those with nothing to say.

Jim saw himself as a guitarist and tended to underestimate his vocal ability. True, he may not have possessed any phenomenal technique as a singer, but he could outsing most of the screamers and shouters who were his contemporaries. 'I just wish I could sing really nice, but I know I can't sing', he once told me. 'I just feel·the words out. I try all right to hit a pretty note, but it's hard. I'm more of an entertainer and performer than a singer.'

But Jimi had a great style to his singing that could be sly, hip and in the vernacular — funky. Sometimes he was flat, or slightly strangled. But often he seemed markedly conscientious in his desire to sing well, and his occasional lapse into a semi-talking style gave an added dimension of humour. There was a tremendous attraction in Jimi's voice, an odd mixture of cool assurance and a nervous stammer.

For a man who staked his claim to fame as a rock guitarist, he wrote an extraordinary number of good songs. While his vocal mannerisms were influenced by Bob Dylan, his first lyrics were influenced by his tastes in science fiction and LSD. One of his earliest compositions, 'Stars That Play With Laughing Sam's Dice,' could be abbreviated to STP — LSD and interpreted as a paean to hallucinogenics. 'I hope you're enjoying the journey, I am,' sings a breathless Jimi conducting a trip to the Milky Way. 'No throwing cigarette butts out the window'.

But the acid trip in his writing was not to last, and was not greatly significant. Jimi's later poetry was original and imaginative without recourse to chemical stimulation. he could be obscure for its own sake, but he could also assume the role of narrator as on 'Highway Chile' and on sexual teasers like 'Fire' and 'Foxy Lady'. Often his lyrics were concerned with a search for someone or something better, but his most revealing writing was about himself, best exemplified by 'My Friend' on *Cry of Love*.

Jimi wrote in rather solitary fashion which was probably one of the underlying causes of the break up of the Experience. Although one or two Noel Redding compositions were recorded by the band, they were more or less token gestures. And apart from 'Wild Thing', the number popularised by the Troggs, and Dylan's 'All Along The Watchtower', there were few non-Hendrix compositions performed.

Most of the songs were evolved in recording studios where words and music could be put down on separate tracks, overlaid, cut and dubbed in a magnetic tapestry. The stage at 'live' gigs was the testing ground for Hendrix' music. Here he had to live up to legend, myth, fantasy and fact. It was on stage where he had to battle with acoustics, electricity, people backstage and people out front. Not all his songs proved suitable for a stage act, and of course one of the fatal problems of the Experience was the demand by audiences for old, familiar material, a cause of much frustration.

To combine the facilities of the studio and the spontaneity of the 'live' gig was doubtless Jimi's quest as it is of most of today's thinking rock bands. He did not have the benefit of the sophistication of their audio equipment. He had mainly volume, and his array of foot pedals.

Like most self-taught musicians, Jimi was not over-conscious of rules about guitar-playing, and while his technique was in no way a fake he was not afraid to utilise effects in a way some saw as mere trappings. For all their endless good taste and finely developed plectrum ability, Jimi was to make many of the accepted modern jazz guitarists sound flat, sterile and emasculated.

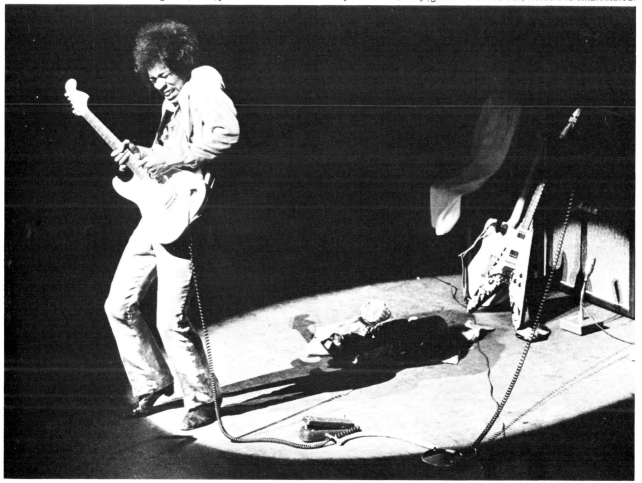

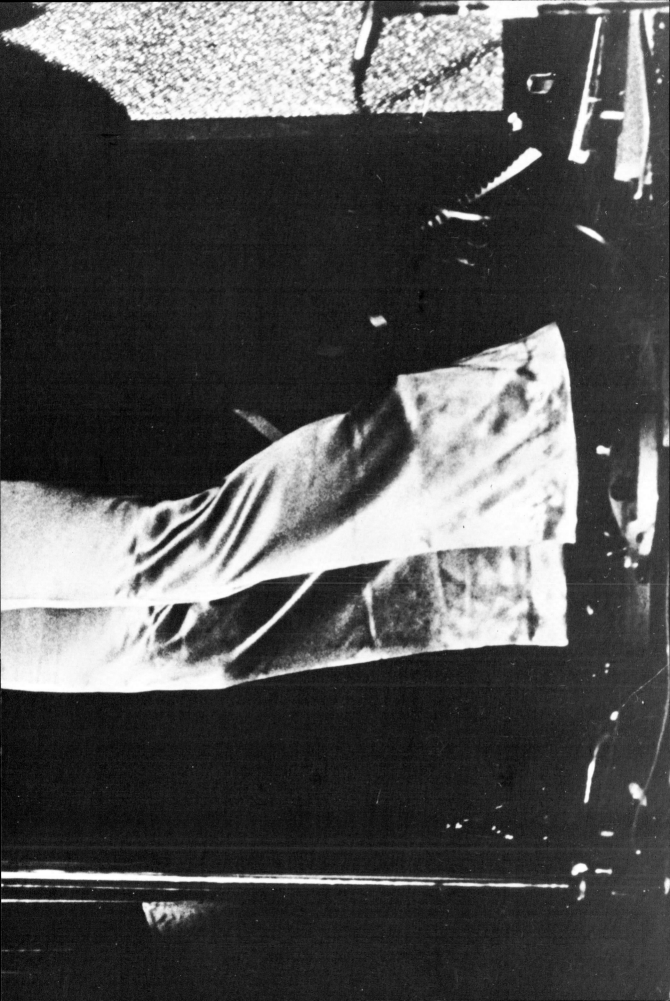

Others had used fuzz-box and wah-wah pedals before him, but Jimi used their howls and screams like a symphony for the technological age. Said Jimi once: 'We don't use gimmicks for their own sake. I get accused of being electronically hung up, but what happens there on stage is what I do myself.'

A lot of equipment was developed especially for him including the Univibe, a device which simulates a rotating speaker sound with a wide-band variable speed control. It was designed for use with electric organs but was adapted for Jimi and it became a vital weapon in his effects armoury.

Jimi didn't rely on the pedals as a crutch for incompetence as those suspicious of rock musicians will charge. He used them in a legitimate technique which was to influence a whole range of guitarists, including younger jazz players and rock guitarists all over the world.

Possibly the greatest stumbling block to acceptance among the sceptics (whether such acceptance matters anyway), was Jimi's reputation as a smasher of guitars. Much of the reputation of the Experience as showmen was borrowed from another group — the Who. Pete Townshend had long previously established as his trademark the ability to wreck a Rickenbacker at the climax of a performance. 'Auto-destruction' was the neat label used to make significant Pete's admitted frustration at his playing. The Who were freaking-out long before the phrase had transmitted across the Atlantic to England.

Hendrix had never heard of the Who before he came to England — only Eric Clapton. Yet many observers could see the Who influence on the Experience's act. The guitar burning and breaking that Jimi indulged in at the start of his career in England was to remain a strong factor in his public image.

In truth, guitars were probably Jimi's most precious possession. The theft of a favourite guitar was more of a tragedy than an inconvenience. He had about eight guitars including a Fender Stratocaster, Gibson Flying Angel, double-neck six and twelve string Gibsons, a Rickenbacker bass and two eight string bass guitars. (He used an eight string bass on 'Spanish Castle Magic', and both models were made by Hagstrom of America.)

In an attempt to explain the guitar smashing routine, Jimi said: 'One time I was rolling around the stage and I fell off into the crowd. I tried to get back but the crowd was pressing in so I threw the guitar back. I didn't mean to break it, but when you throw a guitar it breaks. Once I couldn't get what I wanted out of an amplifier so I kicked it and kicked it. We just try not to bore ourselves — and hope the audience likes it.'

'Sometimes I jump on the guitar. Sometimes I grind the strings up against the frets. The more it grinds, the more it whines. Sometimes I rub up against the amplifier. Sometimes I play the guitar with my teeth, or with my elbow. I can't remember all the things I do.'

The dental routine — apparently playing guitar with his teeth — was to be the cause of much heated discussion in readers' correspondence columns of the musical press.

'My friend reckons he don't play with his teeth, he's pressing the strings with his fingers to get the notes,' Reg Cattermole, Staines, Middlesex. This was frequently the reaction among his more sceptical fans. Jimi gave his own version of how such incisive qualities developed.

'The idea of doing that came to me in a town in Tennessee. Down there you have to play with your teeth or else you get shot. There's a trail of broken teeth all over the stage. It was another way of letting out things, and you have to know what you are doing or you might hurt yourself. The trouble was audiences took it as something they must see or they didn't enjoy the show. So I don't do it too much anymore. We don't do too much of anything anymore, except play music.'

The first posthumously released album, *Cry of Love,* illustrates the new direction in which Jimi wanted to go, and the change he wanted to make in his stage act. It would have guaranteed him a more sophisticated audience interested in a creative talent, not just one that paid homage to a fading image. The last track, 'My Friend', was impressive in its dry, laconic humour. Jimi states that his true friend only reveals himself when he takes a look in the mirror. The song certainly confirmed the belief that Jimi was consistently suspicious of others and found it difficult to find friends he could trust. As the song romps along in its easy, loping way, intoxicated voices in the background shout encouragement, recalling Dylan's 'Rainy Day Women Nos. 12 & 35.' Jimi feigns surprise that his only friend 'looks, thinks and acts just like himself.' But instead of a gloomy complaint, the cheerful mood that prevails is supremely ironic. It was tempting to hope that Jimi would have gone on to write more in this communicative direct style. There is no doubt he had a lot more to say.

With greater care taken by himself and others, Jimi would have been an even greater musician. Yet the experiences he went through made him such a vibrant living artist. It was the combination of early restrictions and hard won freedom that finally wrought such an erratic flow of pent-up, creative genius. The balance between his appetite for life and over-indulgence was the balance between energising his natural talent and snuffing it out. That talent was beginning to flow again, just before his death.

His music did not speak for others and he was not a self-identifying figure in the way that other rock heroes were. He was too individual and flamboyant for audiences ever to imagine themselves as Jimi Hendrix in the way that they could see themselves as Bob Dylan. And while thousands of young guitarists could emulate Eric Clapton, and identify with his role, Jimi was further out than most could conceive.

Whether his environment helped create him, or destroy him, he has left a rich legacy, preserved in the sort of memorial that Jimi himself would have preferred — his records, his songs and music.

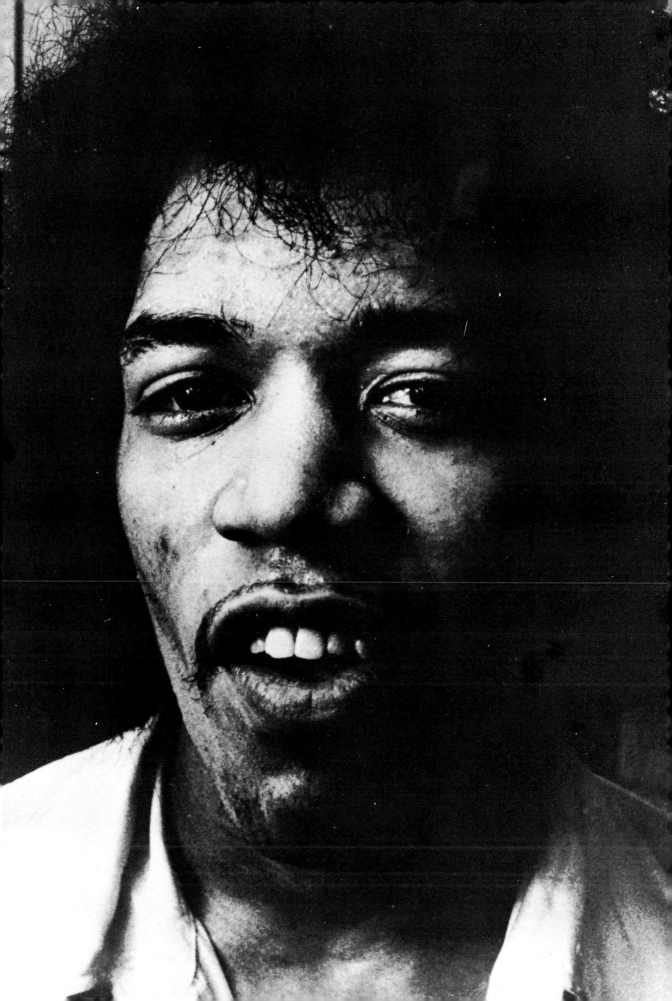

'Call Me Helium'

Just after his Isle of Wight appearance, and a few weeks before his death, Jimi gave an interview with Keith Altham in London, one of the last, in which he tried to explain the changes he had been through, talked about the future, and added a few gentle send-ups. What was the reason for the 'new, subdued Jimi Hendrix?' (Pause for laughter from Jimi).

'I don't know really. I've been going through certain changes. I guess it's something else for people to talk about. It's got to be quiet for a while. I just tried to do the gigs and stay away for a while. I was changing and getting into heavier music. It was getting unbearable with three pieces. And I wanted to expand on this. But I think I'll get back to three pieces again, and get another bass player and be loud again. No!'

Was he worried the subdued approach would lose him mystique?

'Everybody goes through these changes — like the first time around. I see Mountain and these new groups, Cactus and whatever. You see new pictures of them and now their hair is getting longer, and they wear more jewellery and strangle themselves with beads, but I just did that because I felt like I was being too loud or something. I wanted to hype up on the visual thing so I could be listened to. I don't know if I was or not. After a while I started getting aware too much of what was going down. It started bringing me down, and this is why I started cutting my hair a bit, rings disappearing, one by one. Ha, ha. No, it wasn't a publicity hype to start with. It was mainly my own scenes. I'd say maybe I should smash a guitar or something tonight. And they'd say "Yeah, yeah!" And I'd say, "Do you really think I should?" And they'd say, "Yeah, that'll be cool." So I worked up enough anger so I could do it. But I didn't think too much of the hype scene and all that, but the things I did — it was fun. I didn't know it was anger until they told me that it was — all that destruction. Maybe everybody should have like a room, where they can get rid of all their inhibitions. So my room was a stage.'

How did Jimi feel about his Isle of Wight performance? Was he satisfied with the results?

'Well there was some mix up there, and at the time it got so confused, I didn't really have a chance to base my future on that one gig. Except when I played "God Save the Queen". I was happy just to play there. It's hard to say what I'll do next. I'd like to have a small group, and a large one, and maybe go touring with one of them. We're trying to get another tour of England together, and that's definitely a call for a new bass player. Billy Cox has split. I could get really wild again. It's hard to know what people want around here sometimes, but I can't feel anything right now because there's a few phases that's happened. And so I have to lay back, and think about it all.'

Did Jimi feel he was properly appreciated as a song writer? Did he feel his image got in the way?

'Probably that's a good thing, because I'm still trying to get my writing together. All I write is what I feel, that's all. And I don't really round it off too good, it's almost naked. And the words are so bland that nobody can get into them. And when we play — flip around and flash around — people just see what their eyes see, and forget about their ears. I'm trying to do too many things at the same time, which is my nature. I just hate to be in one corner, I hate to be put as only a guitar player, or only a songwriter, or only a tap dancer! I like to move around.'

What did Jimi want to turn people on to, apart from his music. Were there any moral or political overtones to his writing?

'I just like people to get easier in their minds, because there are too many heavy songs nowadays. Music has been getting too heavy, almost to the state of unbearable. When things get too heavy, just call me helium, the lighest known gas to man . . .'

Did Jimi feel popular music was going to change the world, or was it a reflection of the world?

'It's a reflection. See, the reflection is like the blues. And there's this other kind of music that's trying to come up, it's not sunshine music necessarily, it's more an easier type of thing with less worries and more meaning to it. You don't have to be singing about love all the time in order to give love.'

What would Jimi like to see changed in the world?

'Oh, I don't know. More colour in the streets probably. Whatever happens, it should have a chance to be brought into the open. If it's a new idea, a new invention or a new way of thinking, it should at least be brought into the open. We shouldn't have to keep carrying the same old burdens around. You have to be a freak in order to be different. And them freaks are very prejudiced. You have to talk in a certain way in order to be with them. And in order to be with the others, you have to wear your hair short and wear a tie. So we're trying to make a third world happen . . . But I guess a person has to change himself in order to be a living example of what he's singing about. In order to change the world, you have to get your head together first.'

Was Jimi's music angry, raging against the Establishment?

'Oh, this is not raging music, but if it was up to me there would be no such thing as an Establishment. It's some sort of a blues – that's all I'm singing about. It's today's blues.'

Did Jimi have any politics?

'Not really. I was ready to get into all that, but everybody goes through those stages too. It all comes out in the music. We had one song called "Straight Ahead" and it says like "Power to the people, freedom to the soul, pass it on to the young and old, we don't give a damn for heroes, short or long, communications coming on strong." '

It has been said he invented psychedelic music . . .

'Ha ha . . . the mad scientist. I'll tell you the truth. *Are You Experienced* – I heard that just recently, and it seemed like I must have been high or something. When I heard it I said, "Damn, I wonder where my head was at when I said all those things?" I don't consider that the invention of psychedelic music, it was just asking a lot of questions. The way I write things, they are just a clash between reality and fantasy. You have to use fantasy to show different sides to reality.'

What recordings by the Experience were left in the can and what was coming next?

'Well I think we're going to have this thing called Horizon, and we have this other one called "Astral Man", talking about living in peace of mind, and so on. Are these psychedelic? I don't know what that word means. Really. Does it mean you say one thing and mean another? Or can you get three different meanings out of one thing? Is that what they say?'

Doesn't it have LSD connotations?

'Oh you mean strictly LSD? You mean that type of consciousness? Oh, right. Oh you have to give 'em a little bit to dream on so you can hear it over again. Dreams come from different moods, you know.'

Did Jimi feel he had enough money to live comfortably without making anymore?

'Ah, I don't think so. Because I want to wake up in the morning and just roll out of my bed into an indoor swimming pool, and then swim to the breakfast table, come up for air and maybe get a drink of orange juice, and then swim into the bathroom, and y'know . . . have a shave. No, I don't want to live luxuriously. Is that luxurious? Maybe I'll live in a tent, overhanging a mountain stream.'

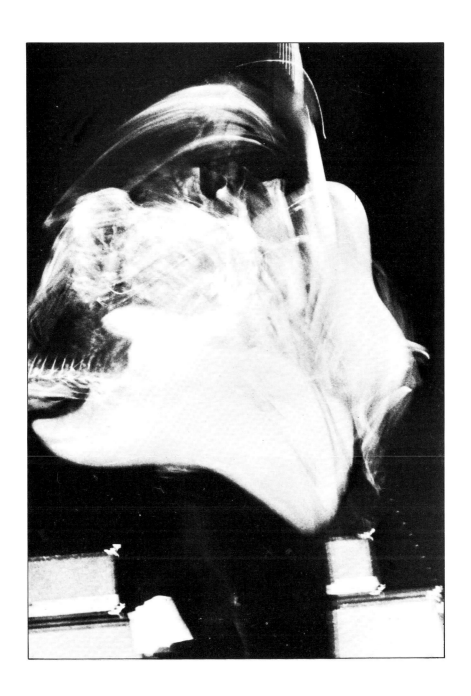

Application Number. 3.019......

The fee for this certificate is 8s. 0d.
When application is made by post, a
handling fee is payable in addition.

QDX 00412·

CERTIFIED COPY   OF AN ENTRY

DEATH

| | Entry No. | **7** |

Registration district   Kensington

Sub-district   St. Mary Abbots

Administrative area
Royal Borough of Kensington
and Chelsea

1. Date and place of death   *Eighteenth September 1970*
St. Mary Abbots Hospital Kensington

2. Name and surname   *Jimi HENDRIX otherwise James Marshall HENDRIX*

3. Sex *Male*

4. Maiden surname of woman who has married   —

5. Date and place of birth   *27th November 1942*
United States of America

6. Occupation and usual address   *a musician,*
507/508 Cumberland Hotel
Great Cumberland Place, Marylebone.

7.(a) Name and surname of informant   *Certificate received from G. Thurston.* **(b) Qualification** *Coroner for Inner West London. Inquest held 28th September 1970*

(c) Usual address

8. Cause of death

Inhalation of vomit
Barbiturate intoxication (quinalbarbitone)
Insufficient evidence of circumstances
open verdict

9. I certify that the particulars given by me above are true to the best of my knowledge and belief _____ Signature of informant

10. Date of registration   *Twentyninth September 1970*

11. Signature of registrar   *E. M. Fisher Registrar*

Form A504AX (S.308676) Dd 633663 5,000 3/69 Hw–RI–58

CERTIFIED to be a true copy of an entry in the certified copy of a register of Deaths in the District above mentioned. Given at the GENERAL REGISTER OFFICE, SOMERSET HOUSE, LONDON, under the Seal of the said Office on *8th September* 19.72.

Friday The Eighteenth

When Jimi died, the first assumption was that he had succumbed to an overdose of drugs. Another was that he had taken his own life.

Jimi died on Friday September 18, 1970, after he had collapsed at his girl friend Monika Danneman's flat beneath a hotel in Notting Hill, London. He was taken to St. Mary Abbott's hospital, Kensington, and was dead on arrival.

At an inquest opened at Westminster on September 23, the Coroner, Dr. Gavin Thurston, called for an adjournment until a post mortem test had been made. Later, on September 28, the pathologist, Prof. Donald Teare, said that the cause of death was an inhalation of vomit due to barbiturate intoxication. Hendrix was not a drug addict. He had taken too many sleeping tablets. An open verdict was recorded and there was no firm evidence that Jimi had tried to commit suicide.

Monika Danneman, his beautiful German girl friend, was a skating instructress he had met in Dusseldorf in 1969. Jimi had several girl friends, but Monika had shared his last hours. She says they had talked of marriage.

Jimi had been booked into the Cumberland Hotel on September 6. On the Wednesday before his death he had been to the Ronnie Scott jazz club in Frith Street, Soho, to see and jam with Eric Burdon's new group, War. Said Eric, about this last jam session: 'I knew Jimi would be in town during the week. I had an excited feeling that he would come and play with us, and while we were at the club we sort of hinted that we would like to see him there. We knew things weren't all that good with him, but we did our best to let him know that we were there to help him. When Jimi showed up at the club on the Wednesday evening we wanted to treat him like any other musician, so there weren't many words spoken at the start.'

'He started off badly as Jimi the Sound

Eric Burdon jammed with Hendrix

Freak, did one solo which died and was very bad. Later he became better, real loose, but when the break came he wasn't in such a good mood. In the dressing room he said he wouldn't go back on, but after a bit of talking he did, and after some good playing he really got into the last number "Tobacco Road". He wasn't just freaking. He was gelling nicely with the band.'

It was Eric Burdon that Monika telephoned to say that Jimi was ill. At first he told her Jimi would be okay, but later told her to get an ambulance. 'I thought he would be all right, but that was that.'

Later Monika said: 'We got home about 8.30 p.m. and I cooked a meal. We drank a bottle of white wine. He drank more of the bottle than me, but he was not a drinking man. He washed his hair and had a bath. We were talking and listening to music, until about 1.45 a.m. when he told me he had to go to some peoples' flat. They were not his friends and he did not like them. He told me he did not want me to go with him, so I

dropped him off there, and picked him up an hour later, just after three. When he got home I made him a fish sandwich and I took a sleeping tablet about 6.45 a.m. The last time we were talking was about 7 a.m. I woke up about 10.20 a.m. and Jimi was still sleeping.

'He appeared quite normal, and I left him to get some cigarettes. When I got back he was still asleep, but he had been sick. He was still breathing but I couldn't wake him and I realised he had taken some sleeping tablets. I checked his pulse and it was normal, and I thought if I took him to hospital he would be furious if nothing was wrong. So I telephoned Eric — please help me — do you know the address of his doctor? I found the address and 'phoned for an ambulance. It came after about fifteen to twenty minutes.

'The men said he was okay and sat him in the ambulance. I found out later they should have laid him down flat to let him breathe. But they put him on a chair with his head back. He did not die from the sleeping tablets because he had not taken enough to be an overdose. It was not fatal. The reason he died was because he couldn't get air. He suffocated on his own vomit.'

The ambulance rushed him to hospital, but he was dead on arrival at 11.45 a.m. Later police said that nine sleeping tablets were missing from a bottle in Monika's flat.

Most of the early press reports on his death suggested that he had died as a result of a drug overdose. One Sunday newspaper called him a 'Cocaine addict.' Another London newspaper headlined: 'Drugs kill Hendrix at 24.' There were no similar banner headlines *following* the inquest, to the effect that Jimi was *not* an addict and that his death had been due to inhalation of vomit.

The sensationalised Sunday newspaper story talked of him being 'a victim of the pop-and-drugs culture he helped perpetuate.' and said he was the 'prophet-in-chief of the drug generation.' The story ended with the

*Opposite: St. Mary
Abbott's Hospital,
Kensington—Hendrix
was found to be dead
on arrival in the
ambulance.*

lines: 'Yesterday record dealers reported a sell-out of Hendrix's records. Already a wierd cult was building up in his memory.'

Yet the press also carried some well-informed and sympathetic tributes that seemed aware of his musical contribution. *The Times* called him a 'key figure in the development of pop music,' and said 'Hendrix was a gentle, peaceful man whose only real concern was music.'

Three days after Jimi's death, Eric Burdon appeared on BBC TV and in an interview said that Jimi had killed himself and that he, Burdon, was to carry on 'Jimi's legacy.' Elsewhere he claimed that Jimi had left a 'suicide note'. But this proved to be a poem, of which Jimi wrote many. Said manager Mike Jeffery: 'I've been going through a whole stack of papers, poems and songs and many could be interpreted as a suicide note. I just don't believe it was suicide.'

Prior to his death, Jimi had been involved in negotiations about his management situation. Chas Chandler says that Jimi called him up and asked him if he would like to manage him again, but this was never followed up.

Buddy Miles, who played with Jimi in the Band of Gypsies confirmed that Jimi had often complained about his managers. Mike Jeffery denied that Jimi had ever wanted to change management but admitted there were times when he could not 'devote energies' to helping Jimi. In an interview with Rolling Stone that year, he said: 'Both he and I felt that the three way function of manager-artist-agent was quite likely to fall apart because times are different from what they once were in show business. People outside the circle mistook this for discontent, but it wasn't because Jimi was intelligent and bright enough. If he wanted to split, he would have split. As for being artistically frustrated Jimi had an incredible genius about him and the common thing with most artists of that calibre is that they are

Monika Danneman leaves the inquest

constantly artistically frustrated.'

At the time of his death, Jimi's affairs were just picking up again after the inactivity of 1969. The Isle of Wight festival performance had not been sensational, but it had been solid and a great improvement on the Madison Square Garden concert, when he walked off stage.

Billy Cox had suffered a nervous break-down but Noel Redding was waiting in the wings, eager to make a proposed European and British tour that Gerry Stickells had been organising. And there was also the *Cry Of Love* album that Jimi wanted to finish off at Electric Ladyland.

And while other girlfriends tend to discount Monika Danneman's influence or importance to Jimi, it was evident that she had a strong desire to help him and encourage him, which might just have been the right antidote to Jimi's changeable mind and sense of abandonment. Whether he truly loved her or not, she could have been a great asset to him during a time of confusion and

upset.

Jeannette Jacobs, another girlfriend, who felt she was being ousted by Monika, says she only went away from London to Amsterdam the day before Jimi's death because she had been told that Jimi and Monika were getting married. 'I fell for it unfortunately and left the country. Somebody told him I had gone away and the next morning he was found dead.' So Jeannette shared Eric Burdon's view, at the time, that Jimi's death was suicide.

But if Jeannette had gone away, she could come back, and Jimi had been involved with enough girls to know how they behaved. And according to Jeannette they had known each other for years.

So why should Jimi suddenly decide to do away with himself? It may just have been a desire to shake up all the people around him that led Jimi to take an overdose of sleeping tablets. It is common among people who are highly strung, sensitive and easily depressed. As often as not, they wake up in hospital apologising for all the trouble.

Or it may have been that Jimi took some tablets which did not send him to sleep quickly enough, and he risked taking some more. Monika said she usually took one or two sleeping tablets, although Professor Teare said the normal dose was half a tablet.

The Coroner, Dr. Thurston said there were no signs that he intended to commit suicide and there was not enough evidence to show it was a deliberate attempt to take his own life. 'The question why he took so many sleeping tablets cannot be safely answered,' said Dr. Thurston.

Gerry Stickells flew Jimi's body back to Seattle, where he was buried at the Greenwood Cemetery on October 1st. As well as Mr. Hendrix, his wife, and Jimi's brother Leon, mourners at the funeral included Miles Davis, Buddy Miles, Devon Wilson, Mitch Mitchell, Noel Redding, Johnny Winter and John Hammond Jnr.

JIMI'S LAST LOST DAYS

LORRAINE JAMES . . . saw Hendrix make love all night to two girls

"I NEED HELP BAD, MAN." These words, gasped into a telephone-answering machine in an empty office, are the epitaph of Jimi Hendrix, idol of millions and prophet-in-chief of the drug generation.

They were spoken at 1.30 on Friday morning and discovered on the tape when the office opened at 10 a.m.

Charles Chandler of the Robert Stigwood show-business empire and Hendrix's former manager, made a frantic phone call to the Notting Hill number the pop idol had given.

But Hendrix, a cocaine addict, was already near death. "Call me a bit later, man," he groaned.

Within hours he was dead. At 24. A victim of the pop-and-drugs culture he helped perpetuate.

I have pieced together the incredible last three days of Hendrix's life—in which he was missing from his £17-a-day suite in London's Cumberland Hotel.

Millions

Hendrix had come up in the pop world at a breathtaking pace.

One minute he was just another coloured musician in the dives of Greenwich Village, New York's hippie

HENDRIX . . . "Call me later, man," he groaned

EXC...

"He wa 'phone in hours t people. was on the nex about h financia

"The Americ friends Jimi until

"T to Ne West com

wit mi ju ni ca br

Jimi Hendrix dies —'drug overdose'

JIMI HENDRIX singing at the Isle of Wight pop festival last month

Standard Reporter

JIMI HENDRIX, the 23-year-old pop guitarist, died today. He is believed to have suffered an overdose of drugs.

Doctors at St Mary Abbott's Hospital, Kensington where he had been taken by an ambulance, fought to save his life but all attempts to resuscitate him failed.

The hospital secretary said: "We do not know where or how or why he died."

An inquest is to be held.

Hendrix, whose electric stage hairstyle started a trend, had been staying at the Cumberland Hotel.

But his whereabouts during the three days was a mystery this afternoon.

A spokesman for the public relations firm which looked after Hendrix interests and who were trying to save the middle said: He had disappeared.

We have been trying to reach him without any success. He had been staying at the Cumberland Hotel as far as we knew but was booked in until last night as far as we know.

But there has been no trace of him although we tried his friends in the country and in London. They carry a missing...

Hendrix had moved into the

Contd. Back Page Col. 1

BY DAVID TUNE

POP STAR Hendrix died in ambulance yesterda... the way to hospital.

He was apparently s... ing from a drug overdose

Hendrix, one of the sta... the recent Isle of Wight festival, was brought... on stage made in front of countless centre... been found by his his West German girl friend come in bed at her hotel...

Twenty-three-year-old Danneman called an am... and sat weeping bed... he was driven away...

Westminster... said later: "We... overdose. An inqu... ably be held on...

Since Isle of Friend of Hendrix... with Miss Dan... "Jimi spent the ne... friend's bed..."

PIED PIPER O... Page EIGH...

exactly what happe... too upset...

Jimi Hendrix dies in drugs mystery

SHAUN USHER

THE "wild man" of pop, Jimi Hendrix died yesterday. He went into a coma just as he seemed to be getting his first good sleep for several nights.

The cause of his death was not disclosed last night, but it was understood to be a drugs overdose.

A coroner's officer took possession of some sleeping tablets at the flat where Hendrix was staying.

Hendrix, 24-year-old American guitarist, once voted the "world's outstanding musician" by Bri-

SKETCH 19.9.7...

I'm shattered says Mick Jagger

DRUGS KILL JIMI HENDRIX AT 24

JIMI HENDRIX

Evening News Reporter
POP STAR Jimi Hendrix died in London today after being taken to hospital suffering from an overdose of drugs.

Hendrix, aged 24, was taken to St. Mary Abbots Hospital, Kensington, but was certified dead by a doctor who examined him in the back of the ambulance.

... his manager, Gerry Stickells, had ... recently. About three ... their new

man
op
i
ndrix
dead

By JAMES WILSON

TARIST Jimi Hendrix, the ... man of pop, died ... day after his girl friend ... him unconscious.

... is believed to have been killed ... drugs overdose.

... police discovered that sleeping ... were missing from a cupboard ... the girl's hotel suite. Monika Danner ... blonde Monika Danner ... found 24-year-old Hendrix ... in her suite at the Samarkand ... Hotel in Lansdowne-crescent, Nott ... ing Hill.

Hendrix—who played at the ... recent Isle of Wight pop festival— ... was taken to hospital, but was dead ... when the ambulance carrying him ... arrived.

... continental pop singer Eric ... ... year-old Miss

Pop star Jimi Hendrix at the recent Isle of Wight Po...

DAILY MAIL, Tuesd...

Reactions by the London press to Hendrix's death, including the obituary in 'The Times'. Next page: the funeral at Greenwood Cemetery, Seattle.

OBITUARY

JIMI HENDRIX
A key figure in the development of pop music

Jimi Hendrix, the pop music ... can died in London yesterday ... as reported elsewhere in this ... ... Bob Dylan was the man who ... liberated pop music verbally to the ... extent that after him it could deal ... with subjects other than teenage ... love, then Jimi Hendrix was ... largely responsible for whatever ... musical metamorphosis it has ... undergone in the past three years.

Born in Seattle, Washington, he ... was part Negro, part Cherokee ... Indian, part Mexican, and gave his ... date of birth as November 27, ... 1945. He left school early, ... picked up the guitar, and hitch- ... hiked around the southern States ... of America before arriving in New ... York where he worked for a while ... with a vaudeville act before join- ... ing the Isley Brothers' backing ... band. He toured all over America ... with various singers, including ... Sam Cooke, Solomon Burke, Little ... Richard, and Ike and Tina Turner, ... until in August, 1966, he wound-up ... in Greenwich Village, New York, ... playing with his own band for $15 ... a night. It was there that he was ... heard by Chas Chandler, former ... bass guitarist with the Animals, ... who became his manager and per- ... suaded him to travel to England. ... Once in London he put together a ... trio with drummer Mitch Mitchell ... and bass guitarist Noel Redding ... called the Jimi Hendrix Exper- ... ience. The guitarist's wild clothes, ... long frizzy hair, and penchant for ... playing guitar solos with his teeth ... quickly made him a sensation.

His playing was rooted in the ... blues approach of B.B. ... King, but was brought up to date ... through the use of amplification ... as a musical device, and his solos ... were often composed of strings of ... feedback sound, looping above the ... free flowing bass and drums. The ... whole sound of the group, loose ... and improvisational and awe- ... somely loud, was quite revolution- ... ary and made an immediate impact ... on his guitar playing contem- ... poraries.

As a singer and composer he was ... one of the first black musicians ... to come to terms with the elec- ... tronic facilities offered by rock

music and his songs and voice ... influenced considerably by Dylan, ... created perhaps the first successful ... fusion of blues and white pop ... After his phenomenal success in ... Britain he returned to America ... where he was banned from a con- ... cert tour by the Daughters of the ... American Revolution, who con- ... sidered his onstage physical ... tortions obscene. That served only ... to increase interest in him and he ... rapidly became one of the world's ... top rock attractions. Then, at the ... beginning of 1969 and at the height ... of his fame he disappeared and ... spent more than a year in virtual ... seclusion, playing at home with a ... few friends. Early in 1970 he re- ... veiled a new trio, the Band of ... Gypsies, and returned to Britain ... last month to play at the Isle of ... Wight festival. In his last interview ... he was quoted as saying that he'd ... reached the end of the road with ... the trio format, and was planning ... to form a big band.

In direct contrast to the violence ... and seeming anarchy of his music, ... Hendrix was a gentle, peaceful man ... whose only real concern was ... music. His final public appearance ... was when he sat in with War, an ... American band, at Ronnie Scott's ... club in London last Wednesday, ... and it was typical of the man that ... it was he who felt honoured by ... being allowed to play.

JIMI HENDRIX
Not a drug addict

Jimi's
ast
nours

the girl who was
there when he died—

Monika Dannemann cried as she ... last

By PETER STEELE

SIR REGINALD BIDDLE

Sir John Elliot writes:
Your obituary notice of this out- ... standing man dealt fully with the ... factual side of his long career in

LADY DARESBURY

Major Robert Hoare
writes:
How little can this world spare ... someone of the ... of the ... character of ... girls

JIMI'S DEATH

ERS BA
ON

JIMI HENDRI ...
to be remember ...
music. But h ...
likely to be ...
for the surge o ...
ness that has f ...
death.

Since the singer ...
Friday, the most ta ...
of scavenging ...
British

Hendrix On Record

The Jimi Hendrix Experience
(Polydor 184085)
Foxy Lady, Manic Depression, Red House, Can You See Me, Love Or Confusion, I Don't Live Today, May This Be Love, Fire, 3rd Stone From The Sun, Remember, Are You Experienced.
Jimi Hendrix (guitar, vocals), Noel Redding (bass), Mitch Mitchell (drums).
London 1966-67.

Axis: Bold As Love
(Polydor 184110)
EXP, Up From The Skies, Spanish Castle Magic, Wait Until Tomorrow, Ain't No Telling, Little Wing, If Six Was Nine, You've Got Me Floating, Castles Made Of Sand, She's So Fine, One Rainy Wish, Little Miss Lover, Bold As Love.
Same personnel.
London and Los Angeles 1967-8

Electric Lady Land
(Polydor 184183/84)
And the Gods Made Love, Have You ever Been To Electric Ladyland, Crosstown Traffic, Voodoo Chile, Little Miss Strange, Long Hot Summer Night, Come On (Part One), Gypsy Eyes, Burning Of The Midnight Lamp, Rainy Day, Dream Away, 1983 (A Merman I Should Turn To Be), Moon, Turn The Tides Gently Gently, Away, Still Raining, Still Dreaming, House Burning Down, All Along The' Watchtower, Voodoo Chile (Silent Return).
Jimi Hendrix (guitar, vocals), Noel Redding, Jack Cassidy (bass), Mitch Mitchell, Buddy Miles (drums), Steve Windood (organ), Al Kooper (piano), Chris Wood (flute), Mike Finnegan (Organ), Freddie Smith (sax), and Larry Faucette (congas).
Los Angeles and New York 1968-69.

Band Of Gypsies
(Polydor 2480005)
Who Knows, Machine Gun, Changes, Power Of Soul, Message To Love, We Gotta Live Together.
Jimi Hendrix (guitar, vocals), Billy Cox (bass), Buddy Miles (drums).
Fillmore East, New York, December 31 1969.

Cry Of Love
(Polydor 2408101)
Freedom, Drifting, Ezy Rider, Night Bird Flying, My Friend, Straight Ahead, Astro Man, Angel, In From The Storm, Belly Button Window.
Jimi Hendrix (guitar, vocals), Billy Cox (bass), Mitch Mitchell (drums), Buddy Miles (drums, Ezy Rider), Buzzy Linhart (vibes, Drifting), Stevie Winwood and Chris Wood (vibes, Ezy Rider).
New York, 1970.

War Heroes
(Polydor)
Bleeding Heart, Highway Child, Tax Free, Peter Gunn, Catastrophe, Stepping Stone, Midnight, Little Bears, Beginning, Izabella.

Smash Hits
(Track 1613 004)
Purple Haze, The Wind Cries Mary, Can You See Me, 51st Anniversary, Hey Joe, Stone Free, The Stars That Play With Laughin Sams Dice, Manic Depression, Highway Chile, The Burning Of The Midnight Lamp, Foxy Lady.

The Jimi Hendrix Experience: Backtrack Three
(Track 99 Series 2407 003)
Hey Joe, I Don't Live Today, Purple Haze, Can You See Me, The Wind Cries Mary, Stone Free.
Original Experience personnel

The Jimi Hendrix Experience: Backtrack Four
(Track 99 Series 2407 004)
The Burning Of The Midnight Lamp, Are You Experienced, If Six Was Nine, Remember, Gypsy Eyes, All Along The Watchtower.
Original Experience personnel.

The Jimi Hendrix Experience: Backtrack Ten
(Track 99 Series 2407 010)
Foxy Lady, Manic Depression, Red House, Can You See Me, Love Or Confusion, I Don't Live Today, May This Be Love, Fire, Third Stone From The Sun, Remember, Are You Experienced.
Original Experience personnel.

Jimi Hendrix At Monterey Pop Festival
1967
Like A Rolling Stone, Rock Me Baby, Can You See Me, Wild Thing.
Original Experience personnel.
Live at Monterey, 1967.

Experience: Original Sound Track
(Ember NR 5057)
Sunshine Of Your Love, Rom Full Of Mirrors, Bleeding Heart, Smashing Of Amps.
Royal Albert Hall, London, February 18, 1969.
Original Experience personnel.

Woodstock
(Polydor 2402-003)
Star Spangled Banner, Purple Haze.
Jimi Hendrix (guitar, vocals), Billy Cox (bass), Mitch Mitchell (drums).

Woodstock Two
(Polydor 2657 003)
Jam Back At The House, Izabella, Got My Heart Back Together.
Woodstock, 1969.

At The Isle Of Wight
(Polydor 2302 016)
Midnight Lightning, Foxy Lady, Lover Man, Freedom, All Along The Watchtower, In From The Storm.
Jimi Hendrix (guitar, vocals), Billy Cox (bass), Mitch Mitchell (drums).
Isle Of Wight, 1970.

Hendrix In The West
(Polydor 2302 018)
Johnny B. Goode, Lover Man, Blue Suede Shoes, Voodoo Chile, The Queen, Sergeant Pepper's Lonely Hearts Club Band, Little Wing and Red House.
Mitch Mitchell (drums), Noel Redding and Billy Cox (bass).
Berkely Community Centre, San Diego Sports Arena, and Isle Of Wight 1970.
Note: The Jimi Hendrix Information Centre in Amsterdam state that Red House, Little Wing and Voodoo Chile on Hendrix in the West were *not* recorded in San Diego but at the Royal Albert Hall on February, 1969, and that the concert was on February 24 and not 18 as stated on the album, Experience. (Ember NR 5057).

Rainbow Bridge: Motion Picture Sound Track
(Reprise K44159)
Dolly Dagger, Earth Blues, Pali Gap, Room Full Of Mirrors, Star Spangled Banner, Look Over Yonder, Hear My Train A Comin', and Hey Baby.
Mitch Mitchell, Buddy Miles (drums), Billy Cox (bass), Ghetto Fighters, Jimi, Ronettes (vocals), Juma Edwards (percussion).

Early Recordings

Jimi Hendrix & The Isley Brothers
(Buddah TNS 3007 USA)
Move Over Let Me Dance, Testify, Wild Little Tiger, Simon Says, and Looking For A Love.
New York 1964.

Jimi Hendrix and Lonnie Youngblood
(Platinum LPM 6004 England)
USA 1964.

Jimi Hendrix & Curtis Knight
(London SL 3001/2)
New York 1965.

Bootleg Albums

Live Experience 1967-68
Purple Haze, Wild Thing, Voodoo Chile, Hey Joe, Sunshine Of Your Love, Drivin' South, Experiencing The Blues, Hound Dog, Little Miss Lover, Love Or Confusion, Foxy Lady, Stone Free.
Released in California as "Goodbye Jimi" on Kustom Records and also released under title of "Broadcasts."
Recorded from appearances on 'The Lulu Show' and 'Top of The Pops.'

Live In Hawaii, Maui, 1970
Land Of The New Rising Sun, Red House, Jam Back At The House, Straight Ahead, Getting My Heart Back Together Again, Ezy Rider.
Recorded during sound rehearsals for "Rainbow Bridge"
First released in Berkeley, California on Immaculate Conception Records as "Incident At Rainbow Bridge."

Jimi Hendrix Live At Los Angeles, Forum
(double-set)
Spanish Castle Magic, Foxy Lady, Gettin' Your Brother's Shoes Together, Gettin' My Heart Back Together Again, Star Spangled Banner, Purple Haze, Voodoo Chile, Room Full Of Mirrors, Land Of The New Rising Sun, Freedom, Message To Love, Ezy Rider, Machine Gun.
First issued in L.A. as "Live At The Forum" on Abstract Records and in Berkeley, California as "Live In Concert" on Immaculate Conception Records (ICR).
Recorded at Los Angeles Forum April 25, 1970.
Jimi Hendrix (guitar, vocals), Mitch Mitchell (drums), Billy Cox (bass).

Sky High
Red House, I'm Gonna Leave This Town, Peoples, Peoples, Peoples, Tommorow Never Knows, Sunshine Of Your Love.
Jimi Hendrix (guitar, vocals), Johnny Winter (guitar), Mitch Mitchell (drums), Noel Redding (bass) and Jim Morrison (vocals).

The Jimi Hendrix Experience With Ginger Baker
Muma Records California. A blank label recording of a night club jam.

There have also been several other bootleg albums issued in the USA featuring material already officially released in England on Ember, Track or Polydor.
Hendrix also played on some tracks of 'McGough and McGear' (Parlophone, 1967), and 'Buddy Miles Express' (Mercury, 1968) on which he wrote the sleeve notes.

Jimi Hendrix Films

Jimi appeared in the movies of the Monterey and Woodstock Festivals, also 'See My Music Talking' 'Pop Corn,' 'Rainbow Bridge,' 'Jimi Plays 'Berkeley,' 'Isle Of Wight,' and 'Experience,' the latter made during his concert at the Royal Albert Hall, London in February, 1969. Warner Brothers are making a feature length documentary on Hendrix for release in November 1973, which will contain yet unseen footage of Hendrix in performance, as well as interviews with those who knew him and worked with him, and 8mm. film actually shot by Hendrix himself.

Photographers

Printed in England by Commercial Colour Press, Forest Gate, London E7. 12/94 (20047)